THE
ALEXANDER
TECHNIQUE

THE
ALEXANDER
TECHNIQUE

Judith Leibowitz and
Bill Connington

Illustrations by Lorraine Williams

SOUVENIR PRESS

First published in the U.S.A. by
Harper & Row, New York

First British Edition published 1991 by
Souvenir Press Ltd., 43 Great Russell Street, London WC1B 3PA

Reprinted 1992
Reprinted 1993 (twice)

ISBN 0 285 63063 6

Printed in Great Britain by
Redwood Books, Trowbridge, Wiltshire

For F. Matthias Alexander,
on whose work our work is founded.

Contents ∽

Foreword ✍

I was first introduced to the Alexander Technique when I was a student of acting in the Drama Division of The Juilliard School. The point I remember most vividly from the array of new ideas that were presented to us by our inspired teacher, Judy Leibowitz, was that our movement and posture were habitual: they were learned intuitively by observation and imitation, and that wasn't necessarily good. In fact, to get optimum utility as well as maximum expressibility from our bodies and voices, we would have to relearn from scratch, or at least rethink, how to move and speak. This prospect seemed daunting but intriguing to me as an aspiring actor. As it turned out, the technique, which seemed at first inexhaustibly mysterious, turned out to be an accessible and most enjoyable discipline to learn and to practice.

The many obvious benefits that the technique afforded us as actors included minimized tension, centeredness, vocal relaxation and responsiveness, mind/body connection, and about an inch and a half of additional height.

In addition, I have found in the ensuing years great benefits in my day-to-day living. By balancing and neutralizing tensions, I've learned to relieve as well as to avoid the aches and pain caused by the thousands of natural shocks that flesh is heir to.

—KEVIN KLINE

Acknowledgments ∽

We would like to thank the teachers who trained us in the Alexander Technique: Alma Frank, Lulie West-feldt, and F. Matthias Alexander for Judith Leibowitz; Pamela Anderson, Pearl Ausubel, Deborah Caplan, Ronald Dennis, Lorna Faraldi, Barbara Kent, Judith Leibowitz, Glynn MacDonald, Ann Mathews, Troup Mathews, and Sarnell Ogus for Bill Connington. These teachers aided us on our journeys of exploration into the Alexander Technique and into ourselves. We also extend our thanks to those who read our book in manuscript form and/or offered advice: Dr. John Austin, Pearl Ausubel, Joanne Howell, Amy Kitahata-Sporn, Cynthia Knapp, Cynthia Reynolds, Stacy Title, and David R. Zyla. We appreciate the time our students and colleagues gave in being interviewed for the case studies.

Margaret Wimberger was our first editor and saw our project grow from an idea into a manuscript, providing kind words and support along the way. Susan Randol, our second editor, saw the manuscript through to book form. Susan was an inspiring guide who helped us bring about a tremendous improvement in the book with her focused, constructively critical eye. We thank both of these capable women for their help. We thank Lorraine Williams for her patience and her expert illustrations, and our agent Athos Demetriou who showed great interest in our project and provided invaluable insight and advice.

Our special thanks to Jane Kosminsky for reading the manuscript and for the incredibly generous long-term loan of a Macintosh computer.

Introduction ✌

A secretary with an aching back, a mother with a stiff neck, a dentist with a stoop, a musician with pain in his shoulders, a lawyer feeling fatigued, an actor with vocal difficulties, an athlete with tennis elbow . . . what do they all have in common? They all suffer from excess tension and stress.

The Alexander Technique offers relief for these problems (in some cases eliminating them altogether) by getting to the root of the problem: misuse of the body. These and many other uncomfortable and painful conditions often result from poor posture and movement, which puts a great deal of strain on the body. The Alexander Technique is a subtle method for changing habits and attitudes, which releases the body and mind, enhances body awareness and functioning, and gives the body new freedom, coordination, and energy.

Here are some of the conditions that can result from poor posture and movement which can be alleviated by using the Alexander Technique:

backache
neck and shoulder stiffness and pain
bursitis

whiplash
"tennis elbow"
arthritis
disc trouble
breathing disorders
stress-related disorders
muscular tics and cramps
swayback
sciatica
pinched nerves
round shoulders
anxiety and tension

Many people believe that standing up straight is enough to improve poor body use. Unfortunately it isn't. In general, good posture is defined as a static position, but unless good posture can be maintained in movement it is transitory and valueless. "Proper posture" conjures up visions of men in military uniform, finishing school students walking while balancing a book on their heads, or a *Vogue* model walking down a runway. "Stand up straight! Shoulders back! Chest up! Suck in your gut! Tuck your pelvis under!" are instructions you may have heard in gym classes, dance classes, or from your mother. If you try to follow this advice you may look a little straighter, but are you comfortable and can you move—or even breathe? You may be able to maintain this rigid position briefly, but chances are you will soon fall back into your old pattern of movement, or your movement will be tense and stiff.

When people decide to change something about themselves, they usually consider only the part that they want to improve. For instance, if a man wants to correct his round shoulders, he may exert muscle tension to pull his shoulders back. But inevitably the effort becomes a strain, and after a few minutes his shoulders will round forward again. He may decide to do exercises to change the position of his shoulders, but if he exercises relying on his inefficient movement habits, the exercises often won't change his condition.

The body functions with maximum efficiency when all its parts are in dynamic balance with one another. When excess tension is released, it is as if a heavy weight is lifted off the body; there is often a sense of relief and of wonder at how much easier movement can be. This letting go of excess tension helps the body release to its full height without straining, thus taking weight off of the joints so that they can move more freely. The Alexander Technique helps you achieve this freedom, not through programmed exercises, but through a mind/body awareness of how you are functioning in daily life.

The method is not just for people who are suffering from pain or stress; it can help anyone who is interested in learning how to move more freely and easily, look and feel better through improved posture and movement, feel more energized, and explore the connection between body and mind.

∽

The Alexander Technique was developed in the last decades of the nineteenth century in Australia by a young Shakespearean actor named F. Matthias Alexander. He suffered from chronic hoarseness when performing, and sometimes lost his voice completely. When neither medical treatment nor vocal study gave him more than temporary relief, Alexander decided to try to solve the problem himself. After many months of painstaking self-observation in a three-way mirror, he saw that the hoarseness was a result of vocal misuse but that this vocal misuse was not an isolated phenomenon. It was only one aspect of an overall pattern of poor functioning in his entire body. He could clearly see his body misuse in the mirror, but he could not feel it. Alexander discovered that every time he opened his mouth to speak he gasped for air, pressed his head down onto the back of his neck, and compressed his spine, which produced tensions throughout his body. His hoarseness was a result of this excessive tension. He had the same habits for everyday speech that he had for performing, but the habits were more pronounced with the added tension of projecting his voice.

This careful study in the mirror led Alexander to observe that he initiated *all* movement by pressing his head back and down and compressing his spine. It became clear that he couldn't correct his vocal misuse without changing his mental concepts and the way he used his whole body.

The excessive tension in the muscles at the back of his neck, which pulled his head back and down was responsible for causing a chain reaction of pressure down through his spine, with accompanying tensions throughout his body. Experimenting on himself, he recognized that if he could prevent this retroflexion of his head, he would be able to change the way he used his whole body—he would be able to move much more freely and efficiently. When Alexander reverted to pressing his head back and down, his vocal problems returned. He could recognize when he was tensing while watching himself in the mirror and could then interrupt his habit. As his sensory perception improved, he was finally able to feel when he was misusing himself and was then able to maintain his improved body use without constantly checking himself in the mirror. Even after he was able to maintain good body use, he occasionally caught himself falling into his old habit of pulling his head back and down, but he could now use his newfound knowledge to correct his old habits.

Alexander noticed many changes in himself when he could prevent his habit of pressing his head down onto his spine. These included: a release of excess tension in his body, a lengthening of his spine in activity, greater freedom and flexibility in movement, more efficient breathing, elimination of his vocal problems, and improved posture and appearance.

He also found he had heightened awareness of himself on the following levels:

- kinesthetic—He became aware of (1) the feelings and tensions in his body and (2) his body in space.
- visual—He saw his habits more clearly.
- structural—He had greater knowledge of his anatomy and movement.
- intellectual—He was more clearly aware of his thinking process.
- emotional—He saw how he interacted and behaved with other people and his environment.

Alexander worked out the processes of his technique over nine years of self-study, using the tools of deductive reasoning and objective self-observation on both the physical and mental levels. He realized that his problem lay not only in physical misuse but also in the way he was thinking. He found that if reaching his goal (e.g., to speak) was the dominant factor, he would revert to his old habit. When he was able to prevent the pressing of his head down onto his spine, to keep the poise of his head and the lengthening of his spine, he was then able indirectly to achieve his goal, a free voice.

Alexander realized that he was responsible for his own behavior—only he pulled his head back, compressed his spine, shortened his torso, and created the tension that caused him to lose his voice. Above all, he knew that only he could change these conditions. He discovered that maintaining the poise of his head on his spine facilitated the lengthening of his spine, and these together allowed him greater ease and freedom in movement. He realized he could not separate the functioning of the mind from the functioning of the body. Finding a solution for his vocal problems drew Alexander into the realm of the whole psycho-physical being in activity. These discoveries led him to develop an organized method for the control and change of habit.

The habit that Alexander observed in himself —that of pressing his head back and down and compressing his spine—is an almost universal one. As he worked to change his habit, Alexander was forced to work with his mind/body as a totality. It led him on a journey of self-discovery. This journey could continue only if he freely maintained the poise of his head and the lengthening of his spine in movement. This is a journey we can all take if we start where he started— by stopping the old habit.

Alexander's concept of mind/body integration was revolutionary in Western thinking of the time. Today many of us recognize that the mind and the body are so intricately connected that it is sometimes difficult to separate their functions. A person is made of many distinct parts that function together. The way to bring about significant change within the self is to deal with all the component parts, rather than individual ones. All of our activities, whether in movement or rest, involve the mind/body acting in unison.

❧

The Alexander Technique is not the same as yoga, transcendental meditation, massage, chiropractic, exercise, physical therapy, Rolfing, Feldenkrais, aerobics, self-hypnosis, biofeedback, posture training, or relaxation techniques. The technique is an educational process for learning about how to change the habits you want to change. Its objective is to maintain (both in movement and at rest) the poise of the head and the total lengthening of the spine.

The technique has traditionally been taught in one-on-one private lessons. The Alexander teacher communicates the principles of the method through verbal instruction and gentle touch. The teacher and the student work together to bring about change. In order to learn the Alexander Technique you need a series of lessons with a certified Alexander teacher. However, some of you may live in an area where no qualified teacher is available. In that case, this book will explain the basic principles of the method. Carefully reading about the Alexander Technique in Part I and applying the Leibowitz Procedures in Part II will help you gain a greater knowledge of how your body works, improve your sensory perception, and experience more free and efficient movement. It's quite likely that you'll look and feel better too!

The book has two parts. The first part is about the Alexander Technique: what its principles are, how the technique works, how it is taught, and what the student can gain from learning it. The second part is about the Leibowitz Procedures. The procedures show you ways of carrying out movement. They are movements that Judith Leibowitz developed and has taught at the Drama Division at The Juilliard School for more than twenty years.

Unfortunately, the Alexander Technique cannot be fully learned without the guidance of a certified Alexander teacher; as a result, this book is written primarily for those who would like to learn how their bodies are designed, and how they are meant to move with efficiency, flexibility, and ease.

This book is an introduction to how you can learn to consciously control what you are doing in all your everyday activities through the Alexander Technique. It is a process by which you can learn a great deal about yourself and how you interact in your environment. We hope that you will find it a pleasurable adventure.

THE
ALEXANDER
TECHNIQUE

PART I

The
Alexander Technique

Judith Leibowitz's Story ⁓

Three weeks before my fifteenth birthday I was stricken with polio. I was completely paralyzed from the waist down. For about six months I lay in bed immobilized, completely dependent on others to help me move. The doctor told my parents that I would probably not walk again, but fortunately my parents didn't tell me his prognosis. After months of very hard work with a physical therapist, I finally improved enough to walk with the aid of metal braces and crutches. Ultimately I discarded the braces and crutches and used only a cane for support. I walked with a pronounced limp.

I was taught that to maintain balance I had to pitch my body weight forward, so I carried my head and body in front of my feet. I stood and walked this way for a number of years. I felt erect in this posture, but unconsciously had to work very hard to keep from falling forward.

By my early twenties, I had reached the limit of healing that orthodox therapy at that time offered. Because I was a "good patient" and desperately wanted to be cured, I worked very hard at my exercises. In my effort to "get it right" I clenched my jaw, tightened my whole body, and held my breath as I tried to move a toe (I still have no working muscles in my toes) or exercised to strengthen my paralyzed muscles. This tension locked into and helped distort the shape of my body. My head pressed down on my neck, my neck angled forward, my whole body was compressed, my shoulders were rounded, the small of my back was arched, my chest was collapsed, and my body was twisted sideways at the waist. I got progressively worse as I continued trying to compensate for the increasing imbalance in my body. The harder I tried to get better, the worse I got.

My cousin was studying the piano with a teacher who recommended that all her students study the Alexander Technique. Her Alexander teacher was Lulie Westfeldt, who had also had polio and through the Alexander Technique had overcome many of her disabilities. My mother, who was always hoping for a cure for me, urged me to try it. Although I was skeptical, I finally agreed to take lessons and went for lessons, first with Alma Frank, then with Lulie Westfeldt. I had a year of weekly lessons. During my lessons, my teachers helped me release excess tension and stand more erectly. I would complain that I was falling over backward and felt terribly out of balance. When I was told to look in the mirror I was shown that although I was more erect than before, I was still pitched forward. Because I had been leaning forward for so many years, the pitched forward posture felt straight and standing straight felt as though I were leaning backward. It was only through the reassurance of my teachers and by looking in the mirror that I could see that what I felt and what was actually happening were two different things. My sensory awareness was not a reliable guide.

I suspected that intensive work in the Alexander Technique would bring even better results, so I decided to take a month's leave from my job as a research chemist and took daily lessons. The improvement that took place in my body during that month was dramatic. My limp improved greatly. My body began to straighten out of its distortions, and I moved much more easily. As I became more aware of my habits of movement, I began to realize that in order to allow change to occur, I had to first give up my habits. I had accepted the fact that there are no "miracle cures" for polio since polio destroys the motor nerve cells and nerve cells do not regenerate. Although I wasn't "cured," I began to learn how I could change my habits of movement so that within my limitations I could operate at optimum efficiency.

I was excited when Lulie Westfeldt suggested I train to become an Alexander teacher. If I wanted to overcome the difficulties brought on by polio, I knew I had to keep up my daily work on myself; immersing myself in a training program would force me to continue my program on a daily basis. During the next two years my days were committed to learning how to teach the Alexander Technique. I took daily private lessons and a teacher-training class with other students, and I observed and assisted Lulie with her private students. I felt I would never be able to master the intricacies of teaching the Alexander Technique, but my own conditions were steadily improving. I walked with much greater ease and endurance. The physical distortions in my body due to the imbalance in my musculature began disappearing. Many movements that had been difficult became easier. At this point I could pick something off the floor without leaning on a chair or table for support. I lost my fear of falling. Occasionally I would stub my toe and since I don't have the muscles in my feet and legs to counteract the imbalance, I would fall, but I learned to let go as I fell so I didn't hurt myself. I was also able to pick myself up more easily. My mental and physical stress eased, and I developed a more positive and confident outlook. With an improved self-image, I opened up socially and discovered I could make friends easily.

In my second year of teacher training I opened up enough physically and psychologically to recognize my need for psychotherapy. Working in the Alexander Technique demands an objective study of oneself in both the physical and mental spheres. I applied this capacity for objective self-study to dealing with my emotional problems. My progress so impressed my therapist that he began to refer many of his patients for lessons in the Alexander Technique.

I graduated and, with great trepidation, began my private practice. I shared teaching space with a voice teacher who was a dedicated student of the Alexander Technique and who referred many of her pupils for lessons. This was my introduction to performing artists. However, my practice expanded, and I soon began to work with students from all walks of life. In helping my students experience and understand the Alexander Technique, my own understanding flowered. It was and is a growth process for both teacher and student.

After teaching for two years, I traveled to London to take daily lessons from F. M. Alexander. Although Alexander was in his eighties, he still taught full time. He was a great master, and work with him inspired me to delve deeper into myself—to understand more clearly the unity of the mind and the body. Working with him impressed upon me more than ever that the power to change my old movement habits lay within myself. It was only on my return from England that I began to believe in myself as a teacher. I was now wholly committed to the Alexander Technique. Just as a diabetic needs a daily dose of insulin, I needed my daily dose of the Alexander Technique. Teaching the technique provided a way of working on myself as I worked with others.

After two more years of teaching, I returned to England for another six weeks of work with Alexander. Soon after I returned to New York, Alexander died. Both my teachers in New York, Lulie Westfeldt and Alma Frank, had also died. I now had no "master teacher" whom I could ask for advice. Now I was wholly on my own.

The perfection of the human form as demonstrated by ancient Greek sculpture has always fascinated me. As an adolescent I spent many hours at the Metropolitan Museum of Art in New York studying and admiring these statues. I would go home and attempt to re-create their beauty in clay—but I never seriously considered studying sculpture until shortly after I started working with the Alexander Technique. The technique helped me free my body and also released my creative energies. I considered sculpting professionally—I was torn between the technique and sculpture. Both seemed to me to be full-time occupations. I decided that a daily "fix" of Alexander was a necessity, so I confined sculpture to the status of serious avocation. From my experience in sculpture, I was able to incorporate into my teaching a sense of form and three-dimensionality. The technique provides a potential for reshaping the body. Students often tell me they feel as though I am working with them like living sculpture.

I had been teaching for about ten years when several of my students expressed an interest in being trained as Alexander teachers. At that time their only alternative was to go to England to train, so they urged me to train them instead. With great misgivings and feelings of inadequacy I agreed. Two of this initial class of five are still teaching.

In 1964 the American Center for the Alexander Technique, Inc. (ACAT) was founded by four young teachers and myself. This was the first organized school in the United States to train and certify Alexander teachers. The first teacher-training class under the auspices of ACAT began in 1966, and teacher training at ACAT has continued uninterrupted since that time. I was director of the program until my retirement in 1981 and still serve on the faculty. ACAT offers a three-year teacher certification program that is approved by the Accrediting Council for Continuing Education and Training.

During these years I became more involved in working with actors. In 1968 John Houseman invited me to join the faculty in the new Drama Division of The Juilliard School. Since its inclusion in the Drama program in 1968, the Alexander Technique has gradually become an integral part of actor training at Juilliard.

My life is now occupied with teaching the Alexander Technique at The Juilliard School and in private practice, training Alexander teachers, and introducing and teaching the technique in various schools and acting companies. This has given me the daily involvement with the Alexander Technique that I need.

For me, the Alexander Technique is a process that is constantly expanding in scope, forcing me to reach deeper and deeper into all aspects of myself. Although the physical benefits are incalculable, the psychological benefits in growth, clarity in thinking, and the way I deal with my life are equally important. Having an awareness of myself and a means to change puts me in control. I know that I have a choice of behavior, and that is a freeing experience. I know that with the help of the Alexander Technique, I will continue to grow.

Bill Connington's Story ✧

There was very little physical awareness in our family. Unlike other children, I was never told to stand up straight while I was growing up. Sports and other forms of physical activity were not considered important—studying hard and getting good grades were. My mother had studied modern dance at college, and she made sure that all of her children learned how to swim, but that was the extent of our physical life. My father and mother had both been poor in sports at school so we were told, "It's alright if you don't do well in sports. You're just like us." I grew up being frightened of physical activity and thought of myself as uncoordinated and awkward.

The first time I was made aware of how I was using my body was when I was seventeen and rehearsing for *Romeo and Juliet*. The ballet teacher who was choreographing the ball scene told me repeatedly to straighten up. I strained every muscle in my body to try to do as she asked. Sometimes she put her hands on my torso and pulled up, but to no avail. I couldn't understand why she kept singling me out for correction. I looked around the room at the other actors and could see sagging and slumping bodies in leotards and tights everywhere. I looked in the mirror at my own body; it seemed to be fine. I literally could not see the shape I was in.

That fall I enrolled in the London Academy of Music and Dramatic Art to study acting. There was a great deal of emphasis on movement at the school. The faculty firmly believed that the actor's body was an instrument and that to be used effectively had to be flexible and ready to move. To achieve this aim we had movement classes every day—mime, Spanish dance, modern dance, tap, and jazz; we also did physical warm-ups in our singing, acting, and speech classes. Almost permanently clad in black leotards and tights and facing myself in a mirror for hours a day, I began to see the sad state my body was in. I quickly realized the importance of good body use. I saw that if my body was tense—especially my neck and shoulders—my voice, which was so important for an actor, was restricted. If my voice was restricted, it sounded tight, closed off, and muffled. This restricted the emotion I could portray, and the end result was a less effective performance. Tension also led to some unattractive ways of moving, which I tried to hide by moving "gracefully." In other words, I was an eighteen-year-old boy with a tense body, a high breathy voice, restricted emotions, and some mannered movement habits.

Luckily for me, during my second year at the Academy an Alexander Technique teacher named Glynn MacDonald was added to the staff. Her class quickly became the most popular in the school. When a student was having a tension problem in a voice class or couldn't seem to get a scene right in acting class because of tensions or physical restrictions, the teacher or director would often say, "Talk to the Alexander teacher about this." The classes were given in a tiny room in a little tower at the top of the school. There were four oval windows looking north, south, east, and west. For furnishings the room had a few chairs, a table, and a piece of paper tacked to the wall that said, "We can throw away the habit of a lifetime in a few minutes if we use our brains. F. M. Alexander." I found this quote a little overwhelming, but I was willing to try.

At the first class Glynn got right to work with one of the students. She had him lie down on the table, and she put her hands gently on different parts of his body as the rest of us watched. After she worked for a few moments she said, "I suppose I better say something about what I am doing. I don't want you to do anything. What I want you to do is nothing. I want you to leave yourselves alone." I didn't know precisely what she meant, but I was very relieved to hear those words. Eventually I discovered that she was asking us to release all the unnecessary tension in our bodies so that we could function more easily and efficiently. Most of the other teachers at the school were asking us to try hard to get something right, and here was someone who was asking us *not* to try so that the release would do itself.

The classes were great fun. Sometimes Glynn worked on us while we were lying down, sometimes while we stood or moved. At the end of our turn we all felt very light, free, and sometimes giddy. When I left the room I always felt as though I were floating. Unfortunately, my poor movement habits came back quickly after the lessons and I got tense again. As with any kind of study, it takes time to apply the work to your life. Glynn advised us to try "saying no" to our old movement habits in between lessons. We were to lie down on the floor with something to support our head and our knees bent and think our Alexander thoughts. We all did this religiously. I lay down on the floor every day to work on myself. For a long time nothing seemed to happen, though when I stood up after fifteen minutes or so I certainly felt less tense.

One day I was lying down and thinking the Alexander thoughts and suddenly my lower back, which had been arched, fell right back to the floor with a thump. I was startled at the quickness of it, and it helped me realize that I was even tighter than I had thought. The tension in my body contributed to my anxiety. I was so anxious to please and to do the right thing that it was difficult for me to make any type of decision—deciding what movie to see could be a monumental endeavor. As the stress in my body gradually eased, my thinking became clearer and decisions became easier for me to make. The experience with my lower back was important because it showed me that my mind could have an effect on my body in a way I didn't know was possible. Just by "thinking it," I could change the arch in my lower back.

I discovered that I was good in my movement classes. When I could free myself I had a natural grace. The ballet teacher even suggested that I train to become a dancer. She told me, "You have the smell of the dancer about you!" This was a somewhat alarming statement, but I took it as a compliment.

After I received my certificate, I moved to New York City to look for acting work. I decided to continue my study of the Alexander Technique by taking private lessons with Barbara Kent. Barbara helped clarify the technique for me and taught me how to apply it to my everyday activities. She also showed me how to extend my work on myself between lessons. After a year and a half of private lessons I was so fascinated that I decided that I would train to become an Alexander teacher.

At twenty-one I enrolled in the teacher training course at the American Center for the Alexander

Technique. When asked about it afterward I said that my Alexander teacher training was the most exciting, the most tiring, the easiest, and the hardest thing I had ever done. What did I mean? It was hard because my habits were so ingrained. It was tiring because I was working to bring about a whole new way of using my body and mind, which takes a tremendous amount of concentration. It was the easiest thing I have done because the teachers at ACAT are tremendously supportive and nurturing—it is an excellent environment in which to learn. It was exciting because it was the beginning of an adventure, a way to learn about myself and how I interacted with everything around me.

After graduation, I continued to take private lessons and also worked with colleagues to improve my teaching skills. In addition to the students I taught privately, I taught small groups of performing artists at acting schools, movement schools, and universities. It was very helpful to teach so many students. Each student is different and teaches me different things.

Recently I have begun to act again. The Alexander Technique has unlocked a great deal of creative energy for me. In returning to acting I found that my breathing and voice were much freer, there was much less tension in my body, and I could allow the emotions of the character to flow more freely from a place deep inside me.

Without describing all the changes that have taken place in me, two stories will help illustrate my point. Toward the beginning of my teacher training I injured my feet and had to be fitted for custom orthotic devices. I remember looking at my feet (until my training I had been an unobservant person) and thinking, "It's too bad I have such ugly feet. My toes are so twisted and distorted. Well, I guess I was just born that way and there's nothing I can do about it." I didn't think about my feet much during the training.

Soon after I got my certificate I looked at my feet and saw that my toes were straight. I took the orthotic devices out of the closet, and the only way I could fit into them was to tighten my foot muscles as hard as I could. Of course when I did that I had to hold my breath and tighten every muscle in my body. This made it clear to me that before training as an Alexander teacher, I had spent my life holding my breath and contracting my muscles; just holding onto my former tension for thirty seconds exhausted me.

Recently I discovered that the same overwhelming tensions had constricted my voice to an extent I had not realized. I had studied singing at acting school and found that I had a light baritone voice. It was not particularly strong, and my range was small. I hadn't had singing lessons in ten years. I was with a friend who manages opera singers and began singing along with a duet that was playing on the tape deck. My friend said, "Bill, you have a nice voice." I replied, "No, I have a pretty weak baritone voice and my range is only an octave and a half." "There are more notes than that in your speaking voice," she said, "and besides, you're a tenor." I went for a singing lesson and, sure enough, I turned out to be a tenor with at least an octave of notes I had never used in singing before. It was exciting to find the notes that I had always had but never knew about. Only by giving up my fixed idea about what my voice sounded like could I then be free to take a chance and explore my real voice.

When I first read Alexander's quote, "We can throw away the habit of a lifetime in a few minutes if we use our brains," I misunderstood it. I thought, "How could I possibly throw away a lifetime of habit in a few minutes?" I gradually realized that saying no to old habits is an ongoing process. I learned that I would have to throw away old habits over and over again, and that it is a wonderfully liberating experience.

The main tool that the Alexander Technique has given me is the freedom to make choices. I have made bold choices in my professional and personal life —choices that have come from my true self and that could be made because of the lifting of the old bond of restrictive habits. I look forward to continuing to explore other different directions—now knowing where they will lead but knowing I will be able to respond to new situations.

Using the Alexander Technique to Change Your Life ∾

All kinds of people come for Alexander lessons: people suffering from tension and stress, people with back or neck pain, people with poor posture, people whose occupations can cause bad postural habits (dentists, carpenters, computer operators, and mothers, for example), people who need to use their bodies well professionally (such as dancers, musicians, actors, singers, and athletes), and those who are interested in using the mind/body more efficiently and with more flexibility. You don't have to have pain or suffer from poor posture to benefit from the Alexander Technique. People who use their bodies relatively well also benefit from learning how to use themselves better.

The following stories show how just a few people have been helped by the technique. These stories are based on real students we have had in our practices. (The names of the students have been changed.) We have included them to help illustrate what can happen during a course of Alexander lessons with a certified teacher of the Alexander Technique. Each situation and each student is different. Teachers have different styles, and what they choose to do in the lessons will depend on the particular student and what the teacher thinks is most important to work on at any one time. Nevertheless, we think that these case studies will give you a general idea of the Alexander process.

In many of the stories the students go through dramatic changes. Of course, not everyone undergoes such radical transformations. A student may want to have lessons to learn something quite simple, such as how to sit at a computer for long periods of time without getting a backache. But we wanted to show some examples of what can happen through the technique if the student works at it. You too can use the Alexander Technique to change your life if you choose.

KIMBERLY

Kimberly is an executive in an investment banking firm who had excruciating back pain due to muscle spasm and sciatica. At her worst she couldn't walk more than a few steps without severe pain. In efforts to get well she tried complete bed rest, osteopathy, chiropractic, physical therapy, and psychiatry, none of which were able to help her. She finally went to a neurologist and neurosurgeon who recommended back surgery to remove a disc. She remained in bed for two months to recover from the operation. She was persuaded by a friend to take Alexander lessons to aid in her recovery. She now says, "I learned how to use my body differently, which kept pressure away from the area that had been injured. It was absolutely essential to my complete recovery from surgery."

She decided that her back pain came from a combination of stress, tension, and poor body habits. She had stood much too straight and stiffly as a result of bad ballet training. She was so stiff that when she moved she jarred her vertebrae and discs.

My surgery was successful, but I still had my old movement habits. I'm sure I would have fallen right back into them and hurt myself again if it hadn't been for Alexander. I relearned how to use my back. I feel more comfortable and at home with my body, more expressive, more facile. Since I stand and move better, I look better in my clothes. The release of tension from my face and body muscles makes me look younger and feel younger, which of course makes me feel better. I firmly believe that some people can avoid back surgery through Alexander if their back trouble is caused by poor body use. Whenever I hear people complaining of severe back trouble or talking about the possibility of surgery, I march right up to them, whether I know them or not, and say, "Would you like twelve thousand dollars' worth of advice? Try the Alexander Technique."

REBECCA &

Rebecca was twenty-three when she first came for lessons. She had suffered from pain in the middle and upper back for three years and explained that her back felt frozen. She first noticed the pain when she had to sit for long hours in molded plastic chairs in college. Years before, she had been in a car accident, and she had suffered three concussions and strained her lower back as a result of sports in school. After tests, her doctor explained to her that she had swayback, hyperflexible joints, and that the muscles along her spine were in constant spasm. He recommended that she do strengthening exercises for her upper back and also suggested that she take some Alexander lessons.

Rebecca dutifully joined a health club and worked out on the machines and found that her upper back muscles became *more* painful. After three months of working out, she went for Alexander lessons. After discussing her history of back pain, her doctor's diagnosis, and her workout program, the teacher and Rebecca decided that Rebecca was using her body badly while exercising, thereby putting excess strain on herself, which led to an even more painful back. Rebecca asked if she should discontinue exercising. The teacher said that was up to her but if she continued, she should be careful not to use too much weight on the machines, make sure that she added weight slowly, and discontinue any exercise that produced pain. In addition she was to watch herself in the mirrors in the health club to monitor what she was doing with her body and make sure that she was not using too much effort or the wrong body parts to carry out an exercise. Rebecca took the teacher's advice and changed the way she worked out, making good body use her main objective. After five Alexander lessons her pain had been greatly reduced.

Rebecca is an editor at a leading national magazine and spends most of her days sitting at her desk. By the middle of the day her back aches. She and the teacher spent a good deal of time focusing on how to sit well at a desk. Rebecca was diligent in practicing at work, and sitting gradually became much easier for her.

Rebecca is a woman of great intelligence and vitality, but she was very tense. She carried her shoulders high up near her ears, spoke in rapid spurts, and her words were often unable to keep up with her rapid thought process. Over time the Alexander lessons produced a personality change. She became more relaxed, and when the tension in her face cleared up and the worry lines between her eyebrows faded away, she became even more attractive. Her speech slowed down so she was easier to understand, and she made her points more clearly when speaking. Her friends and associates noticed the change. She had lost none of her drive or energy; she had simply learned how to focus it better.

ELAINE ❧

Elaine first heard about the technique from listening to a man and wife describe it on a radio program. "They said you could be almost like a rag doll and let all the tensions drain out of your body at will. And I said, 'Oh my god, that's wonderful, I'd like some of that.'" But at that point Elaine had young children and there weren't any teachers near by. Twenty years later, her children had grown and she moved to New York City. She took a job that she knew wouldn't challenge her, but she needed the money. She says:

> I didn't know if I could handle not being challenged at all; I thought that I would just dissolve. My daughter said to me, "You are always talking about the Alexander Technique"—it had always been in the back of my mind—"Why don't you start it now? It would give you an extra thing to think about." So I started lessons, first once a week after work, then twice a week. It was the best thing I have ever done for myself. Now, at the age of sixty-three, there are more possibilities open for me, more yearning for growth than there was twenty years ago.

> In describing her Alexander teacher, she said, "I had never had anyone touch me in this way. It felt

as though I was not being touched, but butterflies were lighting on me." Every teacher's touch is different—some are light, some are firmer—but Elaine is referring to a delicacy and an unpushed quality of touch that every certified Alexander teacher has. "After my lessons I felt different than I had ever felt before. I had a tremendous feeling of lightness. After my lessons my earlobes became very hot—that came from the increased circulation that came coursing up through my neck and head and went into spaces that it had never been allowed into before. I was captivated. This is the first thing in my life that I am doing exclusively for me. As a family woman, that's something very different."

Jim, thirty-seven, was referred by a friend for Alexander lessons. Jim had been a professional dancer for fifteen years. He had studied modern dance, but had danced mostly with ballet companies. He had quit dancing two years previously due to an injury. He had injured his left big toe while dancing several years before but kept dancing with the injury. The toe swelled a great deal, and this led to a tightening of his whole left foot, which decreased its mobility. He had tried several therapies, which had helped ease the pain to a certain extent.

JIM

Many people think that since dancers use their bodies professionally, they use their bodies well. This is not necessarily the case. Dancers are just like everyone else; some of them use their bodies well, others do not. Dancers (especially ballet dancers) must display a specific type of grace and alignment while they are performing. Often they tighten their bodies terribly to assume the positions they are asked to take to perform the movements of the dance. While they are able to maintain the alignment on stage, some of them collapse and slump offstage—or continue to use excess tension to maintain their erect posture. Jim was one of those dancers who used too much tension to maintain erect carriage. He pulled his chest up too far, threw his shoulders back, and pushed his ribs too far forward, which also swayed his back and tightened his legs. The tightness in his legs exacerbated the tightness in his feet. He did not realize that these things were happening in his body, but once the teacher pointed these things out he worked on himself a great deal between lessons. Over time, Jim's patterns of physical misuse greatly improved, and his left foot became much more flexible. The Alexander Technique helped Jim to free his body and move in a very different way.

Jim is an exercise instructor and a personal trainer, so he began to work on himself, and also began to introduce the Alexander concepts in his classes to make sure that his students didn't overexert themselves during their workouts. His clients find that they are now able to get good workout results with less effort.

DAN

Dan felt very uncomfortable with his body; it felt stiff and tight. He knew that he had poor postural habits, but he didn't know how to correct them. He tried taking yoga four or five times a week and injured himself over and over again by overstretching. A personal fitness instructor worked out with him a couple of days a week, but he encountered the same problem with overstretching. His head, neck, and shoulders seemed glued together. One day in yoga class Dan was lying down on a mat doing exercises and when he was finished he couldn't get up. He had pushed two of his vertebrae so far out that they wouldn't come back. A chiropractor snapped the vertebrae back into place, but because his movement habits were still bad, he had to go back constantly for adjustments. As an accountant, Dan was slumped over his desk during the day. "I felt I was trapped in my body, that I didn't know how to get out of it—I was in a major tunnel and there was no way to break out of the shell that was binding me. It was my habits that were binding me and I didn't know a way to get out of the endless loop."

A friend recommended the Alexander Technique and Dan decided to take lessons three times a week because of the seriousness of his condition. Soon after starting his lessons he stopped going to the chiropractor. "I realized I didn't have to go to the chiropractor any more. I used to be very resentful of going to him. I would go for my adjustment at lunch time, I'd be back at my office an hour later and I would be slumping; by the end of the afternoon I knew I was almost right back where I was before the adjustment. The chiropractor lengthened my spine much too quickly. The speed of the physical change made me feel open and vulnerable. I was afraid because the adjustment was so quick. It's very different from working with an Alexander teacher who may prod and encourage the student all the way, but she never takes me beyond what I can handle."

Eventually Dan was able to sit at his desk for quite a long time with no pain if he remembered that the pain was caused by something he was doing and he took the time to use the Alexander Technique. He is now pain-free. "The technique taught me to trust my body, not to fear it. I always thought I was brittle and I would break easily. The technique empowered me. I've grown an inch and three quarters. I look at myself in the mirror now and I almost look athletic compared to what I used to look like. It's shocking to me all the changes I've made."

JANE ✍

Jane is a thirty-three-year-old lawyer who was referred for Alexander lessons by a friend, who had taken Alexander lessons twice a week during her recovery from back surgery and found them invaluable. Nine years before, Jane had bad sciatica down her left leg and was told by her doctor to stay in bed for three months. The sciatica continued to bother her for a year and a half after she completed her bed rest. She had to lie down often to relieve the pain. Recently she had been told by her doctor that her back was continually in spasm and she also had spasm in her neck. This time her doctor had recommended three weeks in bed. When Jane came for lessons she found it difficult to move because of the pain and the muscle weakness from the bed rest.

Jane's progress was slow and steady. At first any kind of movement was difficult for her, so the teacher chose to do extensive work on the table along with very simple work on sitting and standing. Gradually Jane's neck and back began to free up. It was difficult for the teacher to move Jane's head from side to side because her neck was so tight. These and other movements became easier with time. In the beginning she came to her lessons wearing a neck brace because the cab rides on New York's bumpy streets were so stressful for her neck. Eventually she was able to stop wearing the brace to her lessons.

After a few months of lessons, Jane was able to relax and enjoy the process more. Chronic pain can often make a person fearful and overly careful. As Jane became more able to let herself go and try new movements in her lessons, this new freedom extended beyond her lessons. She looked taller and more relaxed and moved with a new ease. Once Jane was past the most critical stage, her teacher could focus more attention on teaching Jane how to apply the Alexander Technique to her daily life.

Katherine was in an accident, and for three years afterward she had to deal with a progressively disintegrating disc. At one stage she was in bed most of the time. After five months of bedrest, she became depressed and was afraid that she might end up in a wheelchair if the condition continued to get worse. She was in a lot of pain, on a high dosage of drugs and was two weeks away from having a spinal fusion operation when:

KATHERINE ✌

> I stumbled on the Alexander Technique at a child's birthday party right before I was scheduled for surgery. Someone described it to me and I thought, "Oh this is ridiculous. This is flaky." But on second thought something clicked with me and I thought, "Oh, why not try this?" and I went and had lessons. I immediately understood that there might be some way through this work that I could help myself. The technique showed me that I could take some responsibility for my own healing and my own well-being. Since I had used my body a lot in dancing and sports, I realized that I had done these activities in a way that had exacerbated my condition and that caused me pain. It was a very freeing experience understanding I could somehow take charge of what was going on.

At her first lesson Katherine had moments of being pain-free for the first time in months, but this condition didn't last. She decided to take lessons three times a week, and in two months she felt much better. "It was the only thing in my life at that time that made me feel less depressed. I felt like it was doing something." She did not have the spinal fusion operation. For her, the technique has been a growth process, an exciting voyage. She has seen that she can have choices in life, and this has given her a sense of liberation.

MIMI ✍

Mimi was a twenty-two-year-old actress and singer who was referred for Alexander lessons by her singing teacher, who observed that Mimi held a great deal of tension in her body. Mimi had difficulty feeling this tension but gradually learned to see it when it was brought to her attention. She could then notice her tension habits while she was singing and in her daily life. The singing teacher pointed out that the tension was inhibiting her singing voice—it was tightening her throat, which restricted the sound, and tightening her ribs and diaphragm, which restricted her breathing. The singing teacher attempted to help Mimi with her tension but then decided to refer her to a certified Alexander teacher instead.

The Alexander teacher could see that although Mimi did not feel much pain or discomfort in her back, her back was quite twisted and her lower back was very arched. In addition, one of her legs was twisted because of muscle tension—this was not a structural problem. Because of her unreliable sensory awareness, Mimi felt at first that the teacher was twisting her, when in fact the teacher was helping her straighten out, but Mimi responded well to the lessons and her body began to change rapidly. Within a few months the singing teacher had noticed a dramatic change in the way Mimi stood and the way she sang. She no longer tightened her neck and tensed her shoulders as badly when she sang, which helped her singing. The singing teacher was so impressed that she sent several other students for lessons.

Brian is a sixty-seven-year-old social worker who was referred for Alexander lessons by his physician. He had a troubled medical history: His right leg gave him great pain when he walked, and he wasn't sure why. Physical therapy didn't seem to help; he had had two laminectomies and had tried acupuncture and had had two strokes. Brian had always been physically active, and now the pain in his leg was restricting his physical activity. He was an avid hiker, but now he often fell on the trail.

Brian was forthright in telling the teacher that he didn't know what the Alexander Technique was, had never heard of the method, and was skeptical. He was resistant during the first lesson, but the teacher persisted and used humor to try to get the points across. At the end of the lesson Brian still had some pain, but the teacher had been able to help Brian walk without the limp that he had had for several years. Brian said, "I have no idea what you just did, and I am still somewhat skeptical, but I would like to come for some lessons." His resistance was much lessened in the second lesson, and he became more open as time went on. His walk became more even and less jerky, and after a few months his pain was greatly lessened. He continued to be troubled by falls while hiking, but his posture was much more upright and he was less tense in movement and at rest.

JUNE ✒

June is a physical therapist who was living and working in Florida when she first heard about the Alexander Technique. She had a cousin in New York studying at Juilliard who had a terrible back problem that June tried to manage from Florida. She sent her cousin to a number of famous doctors who dealt with back problems, but they were unsuccessful in helping her. Finally June's cousin called her and said that her friends at The Juilliard School had suggested that she see an Alexander teacher. She asked June what she thought.

I said I had no idea, but I was certainly open to hearing what it was about. I called the Alexander teacher and asked her to tell me about the technique. I talked to her for ten minutes and it sounded interesting. I told my cousin to do it—it wouldn't hurt her. After about two weeks of lessons my cousin was sitting at the piano, pain-free. (This was after four months of pain.) I flew to New York to meet the teacher. I took a lesson, and I observed a lesson. I had a lightbulb experience; it was the missing piece. As a physical therapist I could always get my patients to feel better with the use of my hands, but I couldn't get them to stay better. This was a tool that someone could use to stay better once they had recovered. A few months later an Alexander teacher taught an intensive five-day workshop in Florida that I took. I was so excited by the technique I brought Alexander teachers down to Florida so I could study, and I arranged other Alexander work for them. Every six months or so I flew to New York to take lessons.

June feels that the Alexander Technique is a tool that people in the medical community should know more about. She told us that the World Health Organization considers pain as one of the major hurdles in health care today, and that the method is an excellent way of working with those who have back problems or musculoskeletal pain.

Ken was a very enthusiastic pupil of thirty. He was an actor and worked as manager of an antique store. He was physically fit and had lots of energy. Whatever his acting teacher asked him to do, Ken would do immediately and with all his energy. Unfortunately, in using all his energy, he was also using an enormous amount of tension. Ken was hyperactive—he spoke very loudly and quickly, and his voice was breathy. The head of the acting studio Ken attended suggested to Ken that he could use some lessons in the Alexander Technique.

KEN ✍

During the lessons, Ken would realize how much tension he was using and would give up that tension very well. This had the effect of relaxing him so much that he almost fell asleep while working lying on the table! At the end of the lesson, he would speak in a normal tone of voice with less breathiness and increased resonance, and his movements were not so tense and jerky.

After several months, these changes had carried over into his daily life, and this helped him in auditions and while performing on stage. There was a significant personality change as he held less and less tension. He was much less frenetic, and seemed more open and confident.

HENRY ✍

Henry, a professional writer, had a bad back; it was chronically tense and in muscle spasm. He tried everything—chiropractic, physical therapy, shiatsu, Reiki, Swedish massage, and acupuncture—and it did not help appreciably. He was in so much pain that he could never get comfortable or sit still.

> I was at the last preview performance of *Phantom of the Opera* before it opened on Broadway. It was a very hard ticket to get and it was a very high-falutin' audience. I was extremely uncomfortable physically so I shifted around, cracking my neck, stretching, or moving around every thirty seconds. The man behind me leaned forward and said, "Would you please stop moving." I was so embarrassed by my problem that I said, "I have a fractured vertebra and I have to move," and he said, "I don't care." Things like that happened all the time. It was a drag.

Then Henry's right hand and arm started to get numb, particularly after he had been writing. He was concerned that something was seriously wrong, so he went to a neurologist who ran tests. The neurologist told Henry that his back was in chronic spasm and recommended Alexander lessons.

> From the first lesson my back started to relax because I had something conscious to do to help myself. I realized immediately at the first lesson that I wasn't going to have this bad back for the rest of my life, that I would be able to help myself. My attitude toward my back had been that it was going to be trouble my whole life, and although some days would be better than others, it would never get better. My first

lesson cheered me up considerably. I soon realized that not only would I have good and bad days, but I would have perfect days. People who hadn't seen me in a while after I started lessons were struck by my appearance. They didn't know what was different until we would sit down to eat and they would realize that I wasn't shifting around to stretch my back out like a contortionist. My demeanor had changed. I am much more relaxed. Occasionally I will get tight again, but I now have a way to get myself out of trouble.

Michael is a successful working actor who began studying the Alexander Technique because of general discomfort and tension. He was making good progress in releasing his tension until he was cast in a role that required him to express anger throughout the performance. Although he had never suffered from vocal problems in his many years of performing, after acting in the play for a few weeks he began to lose his voice at every performance.

MICHAEL ∽

One day he came to his Alexander lesson voiceless. He had come straight from a situation that had infuriated him but in which he could not express his anger. It was obvious to both the teacher and Michael that this unexpressed rage had caused him to lose his voice. During the lesson he released the tension that blocked his voice and we discussed how he could deal with his response to anger. He realized that since childhood, when he had not been allowed to express his anger, he had reacted to anger by compressing his throat and blocking the natural freedom of his vocal mechanism. It was this habitual response to anger that he brought each night to the performance. Within a week his understanding of his habit enabled him to change his physical response to anger and to begin to express the anger of the *character* he portrayed without damaging himself.

BUD ✍

Bud had surgery on his back for a slipped disc. Afterward his orthopedist told him that he had an "unstable back," meaning that his back would continue to go out if he overstrained it. After his surgery he developed inflammation of the middle lining of his spinal cord. The continuous pain led to problems in his legs, producing numbness and tingling, which made it difficult to walk. His treatment included physical therapy, biofeedback, self-hypnosis, and several different kinds of medications. One of the medications stopped the pain effectively but made him so sleepy that he couldn't function. The pain clinic gave him a series of nerve blocks and accidentally hit his spinal cord, so Bud ended up flat on his back for two weeks in terrible pain. When he got up, his upper back was in knots. At that point his doctor sent him for Alexander lessons. The technique helped him clear up ninety percent of his upper back spasm. It took longer to help him with his lower back and shoulders. The teacher helped Bud develop a daily program that was similar to the procedures at the end of this book. Because of the instability in his back, Bud will probably never be totally pain-free, but he now has a tool to help relieve his pain. Bud's back went out recently after spending the day raking leaves. However, he was able to get out of it by doing his Alexander procedures, and by staying in bed for two weekends. (Before his lessons, he had to spend three weeks in bed to recover from an attack.) He feels that the Alexander Technique should be part of hospital pain clinics to help recovering patients learn how to maintain good body use in daily life to help prevent patients from reinjuring themselves, and also for pain relief.

Helene won a singing competition and was reluctant to take the prize, which was to sing in a recital at Avery Fisher Hall with an orchestra and other singers. But she decided to do it. At the concert, she was first on the program. She didn't realize how important it was to her or how nervous she was—even though everyone important in music was there. In the middle of her aria there were five bars when the orchestra played alone:

> I thought to myself, "this isn't so bad." I had not been looking at the orchestra or the audience. I had been keeping my eyes on the conductor. I finally did look out at the audience and at that moment the orchestra made an incredible crescendo that I didn't remember them making at rehearsal, although they must have. I felt like someone slapped me very hard with the side of their hand in the nape of my neck. My knees went weak and I could hardly breathe and I thought I was going to fall down. I remember thinking, "If I can just stand up, I can sing." It never occurred to me that maybe I couldn't keep singing. I tried to find something to hold onto. I turned to look away from the audience and toward the conductor's podium to see if I could get there and hold on to it—I couldn't move my legs. At this time everything was in slow motion. It was like looking in the wrong end of binoculars, everything was so distorted.

My eyes went back to the audience and they looked a million miles away. The next thing I remember, someone had grabbed me. I don't remember anything else until I woke up backstage. A doctor there was asking me if I was pregnant and the producer of the concert was holding my hand saying, "Don't worry, you'll put this in your memoirs." I didn't know what had happened.

I realized that how well I sang had no value—whether I was good or bad didn't matter if I couldn't function in the concert hall. I might as well never have studied voice at all. I was in such a state of panic. It was the most incredible thing I have ever, ever experienced; I was literally overwhelmed with fear.

The morning after the concert she had to start a solo concert tour. The only way she could do the tour was by telling herself that the worst thing that could ever happen did, and would probably not happen again. An hour after her return from the tour she called an Alexander teacher someone had recommended. An intensive amount of the Alexander work completely eradicated her problem. When asked how she had changed because of the Alexander Technique she answered, "I haven't changed, I have metamorphosed. What looked like change was potential that was always there and unavailable to me. My fears, my anxieties, and my feelings of low self-worth stopped me from tapping into my natural functioning. It changed everything." The technique affected her life offstage:

My personal life is completely different. What I give and what I ask for in relationships is on a much higher level—much more reasonable, intelligent, and congruent with who I am and who the person is. I don't ask things of people when those people can't really give it. I don't persist in being in relationships when they really don't work. The Alexander Technique is the single most important thing I have ever done in my life. If I had to go back and choose one tool for my whole life, I would choose the Alexander Technique.

How Tension Responses Develop ᔍ

In growing up we all develop a repertoire of set responses to specific movements. The way we walk, bend, sit, breathe, reach, speak, comb our hair, drive a car, and pick up a package is for the most part unconsciously determined. These are reflexive responses carried out with little or no thought. If each time we made such a movement we had to consciously work out the countless neuromuscular responses involved, there wouldn't be enough hours in the day to get us through breakfast. But when these same habits are based on inefficient usage, the very habitual and reflex behavior that simplifies life can also cause many difficulties. Among them are undue tension, excessive fatigue, inefficient muscular coordination, poor posture, and backache.

The programming of these responses starts at birth, or perhaps before. If a baby is born with no physical abnormalities, its muscular development will tend to be efficient and coordinated—that is, if the baby is allowed to develop at its own pace. But the infant may be placed in situations that put undue stress on the musculoskeletal system before it is ready to bear the weight. Imbalance in the muscles may then develop, which may in turn lead to physical distortion and stressful movement. For instance, allowing a baby to sit before its neck muscles are strong enough to support the weight of its head will put stress on its whole body. Placing a baby in a carrier or stroller that holds it with a constantly rounded back is also detrimental. The muscular system will adapt to the situation in which it is placed, and we carry the habits we built in infancy throughout our lives.

Toddlers tend to move beautifully. If you watch them closely, you can see how they lift objects up to their faces rather than slouching over to look at them, how they squat down to pick up an object from the floor, how they reach out to you to grab an object that interests them. These are all natural, flowing movements that should continue throughout life. But even toddlers begin to develop inefficient habits, the most prevalent one being slumping when sitting. This habit is made worse by hours spent sitting limply in front of the television.

Children are imitators and copy the behavior of those around them. They take on the attitudes and stresses, both physical and psychological, of the surrounding adult world. They develop habits of movement and thought that may—or may not—be efficient, coordinated, and free of undue tension. These physical patterns of movement, thought, and learning are the building blocks on which all future development is predicated.

These attitudes, stresses, and physical habits accompany children to school. There they are required to sit long hours at desks and learn skills, such as writing, which require fine muscular coordination that some children do not yet have at the age of six. But above all, the classroom focus is on being a good student and getting the right answer. Often this puts additional stress on an already stressed child and can increase physical distortion.

The child brings the same attitudes and stresses to every new discipline (e.g., dance, sports, music). Physical and emotional stress, cultural demands, imitation, and patterns of thought are among the elements that can lead to a pattern of habitual movement that is inefficient, tension producing, and often painful and which can distort the musculoskeletal system.

In adolescence, when the desire to be "cool" is foremost, some teenagers deliberately cultivate a slouching posture and movement pattern because that is the accepted teenage body language. The emotional turbulence that most teenagers experience in this period reinforces the pattern. These poor movement habits, learned in childhood and adolescence, then continue on into adulthood.

In addition to movement habits, many other stresses affect psycho-physical development. Since the mind affects the body, emotional and psychological factors come into play and can literally shape the body. People have a self-image that has been imposed by family, friends, society, or themselves. A person who feels insecure and shy will project that feeling in the way he uses his body. You can almost see the proverbial chip on some people's shoulders. The Alexander Technique has helped many people feel calmer and more in control of themselves. It does not rid them of their emotional difficulties, but it does change their response to their emotions.

In addition to habits brought about by the psychological/emotional state, physical limitations or disabilities may create movement problems. Severe illness or injury may cause the body to adapt in a negative way. For instance, pain will often cause a person to hold his breath. The restriction in breathing makes the pain worse. In recuperating from a leg fracture, the patient has to compensate for a cast and crutches when walking. This distortion may form a habit that continues after the crutches are discarded. Even after the actual injury has healed, the slight limp that was necessary when walking with the injury may remain.

The mental and physical patterns that have been built up over years can be changed through reeducation. The Alexander Technique is a method by which we can learn to become aware of our unconscious habits and gives us a means to change them.

Mental Attitude ✍

Alexander didn't think learning was possible without what he called a "correct mental attitude." This term may sound a little straightlaced to us today, but we still think a good mental attitude is necessary in order to make significant changes. We define a good mental attitude as one of being open to new ideas and concepts, open to change, being free enough to accept new information about yourself and, if necessary, to make changes. This entails making a decision to take responsibility for learning more about your body—how it moves and functions—and learning more about your thinking patterns—how your belief systems and self-image affect your functioning. In order to do this, you must stop your habitual goal-attaining patterns. Only when we pause and consider a new course of action are we really free to make a new choice. And when we make a new choice we can learn exciting new things about ourselves.

In German, the words for *posture* and *attitude* are the same. In English, the first meaning for the word *attitude* is a position or posture, the second meaning is a mood or feeling. Your mental attitude will be reflected in how you use your body. When you make the choice to have an open mind, to "wait and see what happens," it will have a beneficial physical effect. One of our students made a play on words by saying, "When you are studying the Alexander Technique, it helps if you have a willing suspension of belief." Giving up old ideas and leaving yourself open to the new allows you to learn. Remember, you can always go back to your old ways if you choose.

We have fears about the future, and fixed ideas about how we'll deal with it. The result is that the mind closes, which in turn impairs efficient body functioning. Mind sets produce excess tensions in the body. In a sense, our ideas present themselves in our bodies. This concept has been dealt with in books on body language, but these books are usually highly oversimplified. Just because a person sits with her legs crossed or her arms crossed does not necessarily mean she is defensive, as these books often conclude; she may simply be mimicking socially accepted postures. A person can be quite open and may take on all kinds of positions if she leaves herself free. In our experience, mental and physical tensions are usually much more subtle and complex than the body language books would lead you to believe.

We have to overcome our schooling and conditioning, which was of a goal-oriented or end-gaining nature and often leads to a fear of learning and of succeeding. Instead of being concerned with "getting the right answer," it is much more important to be as open as possible, to be willing not to "get the right answer," to go through the process rather than rushing for immediate results. This involves staying in the moment rather than jumping ahead to the future. Many of us are stuck in the past or worried about the future; we have to remember that the past is gone, the future isn't here yet, and we only have this moment to work with. What happens in the future will grow out of what's happening in this moment, so the more we stay with the current moment, the more fruitful the future will be. This is what the Zen masters have called the "beginner's mind." In addition to staying in the moment, "the beginner's mind" involves the capacity to enjoy your own development. It's an attitude of intense self-interest without egotism, like a child at play, a state of animate, lively unity with what you are doing. It has to do with staying in the moment but without looking for faults in yourself. You don't second-guess how good you can be, or how bad. There isn't time to worry because you are involved with the process of change.

Zen in the Art of Archery by Eugene Herrigel is a book that has influenced many people since it was published in this country in 1953. Although the book is about Zen Buddhism, it is also an accurate description of the process you go through in studying the Alexander Technique. It is an autobiographical account of a German professor who moved to Japan to teach Western philosophy at a university. He wanted to learn Zen Buddhism but was told that he could not learn it in the abstract, he had to learn it in the context of an activity such as the tea ceremony, flower arranging, calligraphy, or other art form. He chose archery because he had some experience with Western archery, but he soon found that he would have to completely relearn how he shot the arrow. The traditional Japanese bow is taller than the average man and very difficult to shoot. Herrigel tried with all his might to draw the bow but could only do so with tremendous tension; his hand wobbled and he could not shoot straight. What he learned over a long period of time was that when his body was totally balanced and free, then he could draw the bow and the arrow would "shoot itself." Leaving himself alone and free of excess tension was the only way he could loose the arrow effectively. Part of the message of Zen then was to leave himself alone, draining himself not only of tension but of intention. This is similar to the Alexander concept of inhibiting unnecessary tightening so that the action can happen naturally and easily. We highly recommend this book to anyone who is interested in the mind/body connection and learning.

You have to leave yourself alone to learn the Alexander Technique. By leaving yourself alone we certainly don't mean that you sit around doing nothing. Of course you have goals, but you give more attention to the means than to the end. By focusing on the quality of the means, the end can only benefit.

The attitude of acceptance and reflection that is the essence of a good mental attitude leaves you available and able to respond to all the stimuli around you rather than anticipating future stimuli, not responding to the stimuli at hand, or playing out old responses to past stimuli. Before you can learn to inhibit your old movement habits and direct yourself into improved body use, it is necessary to let yourself explore. This leaves you free to take chances, make mistakes, make new choices, and follow new paths.

Inhibition, Mental Directions, and Sensory Awareness ✍

INHIBITION ✍

Over the course of our lives we all learn specific ways of reacting to situations. These responses become habitual and are often carried out with unnecessary tension and stress. The need to get the right answer and the need for approval are common goals in our society. Neither of these objectives is bad in itself, but they often lead us to strain unnecessarily, often to detrimental effect. In order to change our habitual responses and attitudes, we must first learn how to give up the old response habit. Alexander called this process *inhibition*.

Changing a habit involves three components: awareness of the habit, inhibition, and mental directions. All three must be present in order to consciously control change. Conscious control is our tool for carrying out the main objective of the Alexander Technique: *to maintain the poise of the head on top of the lengthening spine in movement and at rest.*

We can think of the body as a computer that has been programmed to behave with a set of specific responses. No conscious effort is required to perform most of our physical activities. But if we wish to change, we can think of the Alexander Technique as a way to reprogram ourselves. This reprogramming will only work if we can become aware of the habit, consciously stop (or inhibit) the habit, and give ourselves specific mental directions to change.

There is no way to experience and control a new pattern of behavior without consciously inhibiting the old pattern. Our immediate response to a stimulus is a mind/body set—a habit. How many times have you seen people pull their head down and hunch their shoulders up when lifting a coffee cup? Have you noticed how people slouch over their food when eating rather than bringing the fork all the way up to their mouth? Before these habits can be changed, we need to realize what we are doing, then consciously say no to the old habit. Of course, not all habits are bad ones —we're only talking about changing the inefficient ones! The difficulty lies in the fact that most of our habits are so ingrained that they are completely unconscious. It often takes the objective guidance of an experienced Alexander teacher to point out many of the unfelt habits. Once these habits have been brought to the student's attention repeatedly he may begin to know what to inhibit.

You must inhibit your reaction before you react to a stimulus. Once you have reacted habitually, you have prevented a new pattern from taking place, so the habitual response must be stopped before it starts. Therefore, to consciously control your behavior you must consciously decide to prevent the habitual response. In the Alexander Technique this process is called *inhibition*. When you receive a stimulus to make a movement, your brain sends a message to your muscles. There is a split second between the stimulus and the response when it is possible for you to alter the path to be taken, and this is where inhibition comes into play. You may give consent to perform the action, or you may withhold consent: both giving and with-holding consent are active responses. Inhibition is not a muscular effort nor is it a passive decision; it is a mental decision to withhold consent from behaving in a particular fashion. It is a decision to leave oneself alone, rather than to respond habitually to a specific stimulus. In effect this leaves the neuromuscular wiring clear so that a new circuit can be printed.

Having said no to the habit, you can then say yes to a new response. Saying no in and of itself is nonproductive. Having withheld consent to the habit response, you must now give consent to a different and new mode of behavior. Since you developed these habits, if you have the means you can also "undo" them. The muscles that control movement are subject to voluntary control and will respond to verbal instructions. Inhibition goes hand in hand with *mental directions*, which define what should be taking place in the body during movement.

One of the difficulties in changing habits is the desire to go after a goal, paying little or no attention to the means, or how the goal is reached. Alexander called this "end-gaining." Usually when a person is given a stimulus the initial response is to perform the action right away. For example, when you decide to sit, chances are you will respond to the verb *to sit* the way you always have simply because that is what your body knows. Your body has set responses to verbs such as *walking*, *bending*, *reaching*, *speaking*, and so on. Even if you don't actually carry out the verb there are habitual, involuntary actions your body believes necessary to carry out the activity. If you take the word *walking*, for instance, your body will have a physical response to that word. Most often it will respond by an increase in muscle tension. It is this involuntary muscle action you are erasing when you inhibit your initial response. Having stopped, you are now free to consciously choose another way of reacting.

Let's take another example—that of making the decision to sit. If reaching the goal (the chair) is the dominant factor, the tendency will be to follow your habit. Instead, you must give up the need to reach the goal and involve yourself in the process of the movement. Since the objective in the Alexander Technique is to maintain the poise of the head on top of the lengthening spine in movement, your need to reach the goal (to sit) is replaced by a decision to maintain the poise of your head and the lengthening of your spine as you carry out the movement. A series of verbal instructions are used to define this process. The words are "Let my neck be free, to let my head go forward and up, to let my torso lengthen and widen, to let my legs release away from my torso, and let my shoulders widen." These words are the *mental directions* that are the instructions to the body, telling it what it should do.

It is important to recognize that although the objective is to maintain the poise of your head and the lengthening of your spine, you can't *make* your spine lengthen nor should you position your head. Rather, when you inhibit the pressing down of your head and the shortening and narrowing of your torso and continue the inhibition in activity, this new pattern can emerge. In other words, inhibition is preventive, and you use it consciously as a preventive measure. You can say to yourself, "Instead of following my habit (which I have inhibited) I will let my neck be free, to let my head go forward and up, to let my torso lengthen and widen, to let my legs release away from my torso, and let my shoulders widen . . . and I will continue to inhibit my habit as I direct and carry out a movement."

As you become more adept at inhibition, you will be able to pay more attention to the means you are using as well as your ends. If you are able to inhibit your habitual response to a stimulus and your need to reach a goal, you are free to have a response of your choice. For example, if your habit is to lean forward from the waist when sitting at a table (which is hard on the lower back), you can inhibit that habit—which will free you to carry out your choice to move from your hip joints when you lean forward. Since life situations are never quite the same, you can free yourself to have a reaction that is appropriate to a particular situation. The quality of your means will determine the quality of your end. Obviously, it is impractical to stop and redirect each activity. But when you choose, you can work at it, and with repetition the new pattern can become strong enough to replace the old habit.

Inhibition is the non-doing of a habit. It is a skill that can be learned and developed to help free us of habit. Until we can give up our habits, we have no free choice. Inhibition gives us that capacity. It can help with more than physical habits. We all have habitual responses to mental/emotional activities such as concentration, anxiety, and anger. Since the mind and body are intricately connected and cannot be separated, all of our so-called mental and physical habits are connected.

The insights we gain from an objective study of our responses to inhibition and verbal directions occur on all levels. The ability to inhibit or withhold consent to a particular behavior can be a liberating experience. This concept has profound and far-reaching philosophical implications if you choose to explore them. True freedom comes from the capacity to choose a pattern of behavior independent of the chains of habit—to make a choice unburdened by the past.

Once we have inhibited the habitual response, mental directions define what should be taking place in the body and lead us through change. Many people tend to contract their neck muscles, which pulls the head back and down on the neck. This can cause a chain reaction of compression throughout the body. Inhibition and mental directions can help change this pattern. As stated before, the directions are "Let my neck be free, to let my head go forward and up, to let my torso lengthen and widen, to let my legs release away from my torso, and let my shoulders widen." The words will come to have a deeper meaning as you experience their effect on your body.

To explain the directions more clearly, we have broken them into parts. However, we want to emphasize that when you are thinking them you should think of the *whole* sentence. Don't break your body into parts; get it to work as a coordinated whole.

Let's take the first phrase:

Let my neck be free . . .

The first and most important word in this phrase is *let*. There is nothing you can *do* to free a muscle. If you try to release by deliberately *moving* your neck, you will create more tension. You will move your neck in accord with your old habit because that's all your body knows how to do. Instead, *think*—send the message from your brain through your nervous system to your muscles. When you think of freeing your neck, you are letting go of the muscular tensions that pull the back of your head down onto your neck, or cervical spine, and compress it, often increasing the spine's forward curve.

to let my head go forward and up . . .

Forward does not mean putting your head forward in space, nor are we talking about a fixed position for your head. Instead, we are talking about a balance of your head on top of your spine. When your neck muscles are tight, they tend to pull your head back and down. If the tension at the base of your skull is released, your head will naturally rotate slightly forward from that point—it can then release in an upward direction. It will be poised and free and able to move in any direction within its range.

to let my torso lengthen and widen . . .

This phrase also begins with the words *to let*, reminding us that the goal is achieved through thought rather than muscular effort. Having given up the compression of your head into your spine, you give your spine the potential to release into its full length. Your skeletal muscles can release into their optimal balanced length throughout your torso, and your spine can reach its normal length and curvature. Widening refers to a release of muscles away from the central axis of your spine out to your sides. Lengthening and widening creates a release into the full dimensions of your three-dimensional torso. Lengthening and widening function together.

to let my legs release away from my torso . . .

Your torso (including your pelvis) releases in the direction of your head. At the same time your legs release in the opposite direction, away from pelvis. The leg muscles will lengthen toward the floor when you inhibit pulling them and into the hip joints.

and let my shoulders widen . . .

When the tension in your shoulders releases, your shoulders tend to widen out to the sides rather than rounding forward or pulling back in a military fashion.

Let's return to the whole sentence: "Let my neck be free, to let my head go forward and up, to let

THE ALEXANDER TECHNIQUE

my torso lengthen and widen, to let my legs release away from my torso, and let my shoulders widen."

When inhibiting and directing, you facilitate the release of excess muscular tension that compresses your skeleton and internal organs. The release of excess muscle tension brings about the subtle lengthening of the spine. You can then reach your full dimensions.

The Alexander directions define what should be taking place in your body. But words have associated verbal, kinesthetic, visual, structural, psychological, and philosophical meanings, all of which come into play when you are thinking them. It is therefore important to understand these instructions on as many levels within yourself as you can. In directing something to take place in your body, the quality of your response depends not only on your physical state, but also on your understanding of the words and the process. These directions work together with inhibition to bring about the objective of the Alexander Technique: to maintain the poise of the head on top of the lengthening spine. This brings about a dynamic balance of opposing parts that is freely maintained in movement and at rest.

Alexander could clearly see his physical habits in the mirror, but he could not feel them. His sensory feedback was not giving him accurate information about his condition. This feedback is called the kinesthetic or proprioceptive sense—a subtle sensory mechanism of the muscles that constantly gives the body information about itself. We receive information through our sense organs, such as the eyes, ears, nose, mouth, and skin—and also through our kinesthetic sense.

SENSORY AWARENESS ✎

This feedback gives the brain information about what position and condition the body is in. It also tells the body how much effort is necessary to maintain a position or a condition. Just as sight or hearing can be defective, the kinesthetic sense can also be defective. When we use too much tension to maintain the body's position or condition, the tension becomes habitual and unfelt. Alexander called unreliable sensory feedback "debauched kinesthesia."

The information that the kinesthetic sense gives us seldom reaches our conscious awareness—we are usually unaware of what is taking place in our bodies. As we learn to carry out an activity, whether well or poorly, easily or with excess tension, with good or distorted body alignment, we become accustomed to the way it feels. Whether the experience is based on efficient or inefficient body use, the outcome will feel right or feel easy. Correcting this inaccurate sensory feedback is one of the objectives of studying the Alexander Technique.

Here is a simple example of unreliable sensory awareness: Let's say that a man has a thirty-five-year habit of carrying his head slightly to the right. Although this may be obvious to him when he looks in a mirror, when he's not looking in a mirror the tilt will feel straight. If he looked in a mirror and straightened his head, he would feel as though it were tilted to the left. Unconsciously, he will tend to stick with the old habit because it "feels right." What is felt and how it is felt is measured against the past experience of the mind and body. We get used to a particular sensation and it feels correct, no matter how incorrect it may be.

We are constantly making unconscious and conscious kinesthetic judgments about our positions in space and the tension-support necessary to reach an objective. For example, we prepare to lift something heavy by creating tension before we know how much tension-support is necessary. We mistakenly lock at the knee and hip joints to stay upright, fearing that if we let the tension go, we will fall. Let's retell part of Judith's story:

> When I first started to walk after the illness, I was taught to pitch my body weight forward. Later, during my Alexander lessons, my teacher helped me to release some of the excess tension so I could stand more erectly. I would complain that I was falling over backward and felt terribly out of balance. She would show me in the mirror that although I was more erect than before, I was still pitched forward. Because I had been doing it for so many years, the pitched-forward posture felt straight and straight felt as though I were leaning backward. It was only through the reassurance of my teacher and by looking in the mirror that I could see that what I felt and what was actually happening were two different things.

Every movement we make is based on an unconscious sensory judgment of how much muscle contraction is necessary to carry it out. For example, we won't speak, pick up the phone, bend to pick something up, or run for a bus unless we feel adequate tension to support the movement. Our unconscious judgment tells us that without a certain habitual amount of "oversupport," an activity cannot be performed. These habits are learned in infancy and continued throughout life. We have a tendency to oversupport in all our activities.

We are often unaware of excess tension because we haven't felt the absence of tension. We often don't feel pain because we have not felt the absence of pain.

Having experienced the absence, we must recognize the process that allowed the letting go to take place.

It is the Alexander teacher's job to demonstrate to students how their unreliable sensory awareness is leading them astray and to guide students into different sensory experiences by helping students to lengthen and widen themselves. After repeated experiences, the unreliable sensory awareness begins to improve, and many of the actions and positions that felt "wrong" begin to feel "right." Alexander said, "If it is possible for feeling to become untrustworthy as a means of direction, it should also be possible to make it trustworthy again."

Sensory appreciation is also colored by self-image. Overweight people who lose weight often still feel and see themselves as overweight. People grow up but often see themselves as they did when they were children. The tensions associated with a poor self-image, or a self-image that is inaccurate, lead to locked-in physical stances and ways of moving. In the course of their teaching, all teachers of the Alexander Technique have been confronted by students complaining that the new experience "feels wrong." If their students choose to change, they must recognize that their sensory apparatus is in need of reeducation.

The concept of unreliable sensory awareness is a key one. What we ultimately aim for in the Alexander Technique is an objective, nonjudgmental awareness of ourselves in activity. What is needed is a reliable feedback system that will give accurate kinesthetic information in the midst of activity. In working with the Alexander Technique, you will be constantly barraged by new and odd sensations, which you can only judge based on your past experience. Because your past experience may be an unreliable indicator, it is necessary to have an objective way to measure the new feelings against reality. (When you follow the Leibowitz Procedures at the end of this book, we recommend that you use a mirror so that you can see what you are doing rather than depending solely on what your kinesthetic sense is telling you.) An Alexander teacher and a mirror are objective guides. They give a means outside the self to check on the body's condition. But, like F. M. Alexander, in the end you must develop your own trustworthy kinesthetic appreciation so that you can be independent of both the teacher and the mirror.

As you have more and more correct experiences, your sensory awareness will become more and more reliable. You will be able to tell more easily when you are not using your body well. This will make it easier and faster for you to change what it is you want to change through inhibition and direction.

To change habits, you need to know what your habits are, inhibit them, and then use mental directions to lead you to improved body use. As your body use improves, your kinesthetic awareness is heightened, and you perceive your habits more clearly. All of these components work together to help you institute and control change.

CONCLUSION ✍

Anatomy and the Alexander Technique ✍

An elementary understanding of skeletal anatomy will help you understand and improve the mechanics of your movement. We will discuss a few basic anatomical facts that you must know if you want to learn the Alexander Technique. (Because the mental directions refer to the anatomical structure, understanding the structure of your body will help you understand the mental directions.) We encourage you to use the illustrations to help you visualize the body parts that you can't see, and to place your hands on the body parts that you can touch. Since all bodies are slightly different, your body may not be quite like those in the illustrations; you may also use a mirror to compare yourself to them.

We will start at your head. Your head sits at the top of your spine and weighs approximately twelve pounds (which is about the same weight as a bowling ball). Underneath your head is the curved structure of your spine. Your spine is made up of a series of bones called the vertebrae. Each vertebra adjoins the next at the facet joints, which allow for a limited amount of flexibility in your spine. There is a curve forward in

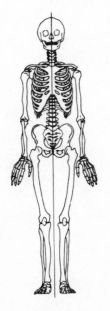

Figure 1

your cervical spine (neck), a curve backward in your thoracic spine (upper torso), a curve forward in your lumbar spine (lower back), a curve backward at your sacrum (the lower part of the spine), and a slight curve forward at your coccyx (tailbone). (See Figures 1–3.) One of the functions of the curves in your spine is to serve as a shock absorption system. If your spine were straight like a rod, every step you took would jar your whole body. The curved structure of your spine helps to promote smooth, fluid movement. The degree of the curves in your spine depends on your body structure—some people have more pronounced curves than others. This is one of the reasons we don't all look alike. A goal of the Alexander Technique is to achieve the optimal length of the spine within your basic skeletal structure.

Figure 2

In between your vertebrae are the intervertebral discs. One of the functions of your discs is to cushion your vertebrae from one another. Nerve fibers come out from your spinal cord through openings between the vertebrae. Poor body use can put pressure on your facet joints, discs, and nerves. This can result in pain.

How your head is poised at the top of your spine is of primary importance. (See Figure 4.) Your head rests on the first vertebra of your spine, which is called the atlas. The joint between your head and the top of your spine is called the occipital joint. Your skull has two rockerlike structures at the bottom. These rest on your atlas. You can rock your head forward or back about ten degrees without moving your neck. If your head moves more than this, the vertebrae of your neck become involved. Your second vertebra is called the axis and has a protuberance that allows your atlas to pivot from side to side. When your head turns, it pivots around the axis.

Below your head is your torso, a functional unit

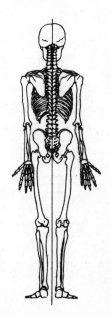

Figure 3

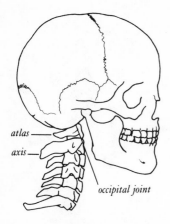

Figure 4

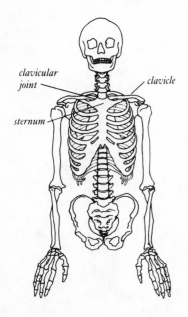

Figure 5

that includes your spine, rib cage, shoulder girdle, and pelvis. (See Figure 5.) Your neck consists of seven vertebrae. Your rib cage consists of twelve pairs of ribs that are attached to your thoracic spine in back and your sternum in front. Your ribs are attached to the sternum by the elastic tissue of cartilage (except for the last two pairs, which are called floating ribs because they are not attached to the sternum). Your rib cage is not a rigid structure. It should not be like a warrior's breastplate—solid and unyielding. Your ribs should expand and contract freely in breathing.

Your shoulder girdle consists of your scapulae (shoulder blades) and clavicles (collarbones). Your shoulder girdle is suspended over your rib cage. The clavicles are attached to the sternum in front and to the scapulae at the tips of your shoulders. Your scapulae rest on your ribs in the back. The only bony connection between your shoulder girdle and your central skeleton is at the clavicular joints in the sternum. (See Figure 5.) Your arms are appendages that are suspended from your scapulae in the back. (See Figure 6.) Because movement takes place at the joints, it's important to know where they are. Since your shoulder girdle is only attached to the rest of your torso at the clavicular joints, this gives you the potential for a great range of movement in your shoulders and arms. The other joints of your arm are your elbow, wrist, and finger joints. The opposable thumb and the rotation of the wrist and lower arm add to the range of available movement.

Below your rib cage is your lumbar spine (lower back), which consists of five vertebrae. This is an area where many of us have problems because there is no bony support in the area other than the flexible spine. Underneath are the sacrum and the coccyx. Your pelvis is made up of three sets of bones that are fused together. It is attached to the sacrum at the sacroiliac joints. Your hip joints are in the front of the pelvis, and the legs are attached to the torso at this joint. (See Figure 7.) Your hip joint is a ball and socket joint—a part of the pelvis is the socket in which the ball of your femur (leg bone) rests. Because of this structure, there is the potential for a great range of movement in your leg. While your spine is a flexible structure, it cannot bend at a right angle. To do that, you must move at your hip joint.

The three sets of joints in your legs are your hip joints, knees, and ankles. Your knees and ankles are hinge joints. Your feet allow for some rotation and are the balancing mechanism on which your whole body is placed. They are multijointed like your hands.

Studying these anatomical illustrations and locating the various body parts on yourself will give you a better idea of how your body is designed. It is especially helpful to know where all of your major joints are. Understanding the design of your body will help you to achieve more flexibility and freedom in movement.

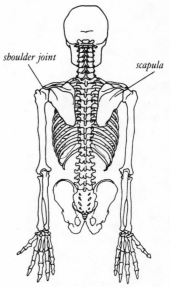

Figure 6

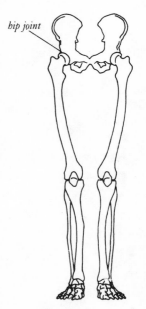

Figure 7

The Mind/Body
Connection ❧

Alexander Technique teachers use their hands to convey a specific way of using the body that enhances its free and efficient functioning. In addition to putting hands on the student to gently guide the body, the teacher gives verbal instruction. Verbal instruction is used to teach basic anatomy, to explain the concepts of inhibition and direction, and to remind students of how to guide their thinking in activity. Both physical touch and verbalization are directed toward the same goal: helping the student coordinate thinking and bodily function into an integrated unit.

During Alexander's time, the mind and the body were seen as completely separate, and the mind was considered superior to the body. Part of what made Alexander's work so extraordinary was that in the 1890s he understood the importance of seeing the mind and the body as working together to bring about efficient functioning. Alexander's great accomplishment was in developing a practical method for integrating the two.

Even today, some people think of the mind and the body as separate entities. We are taught in school that the brain directs the activity of the body. As a result of sketchy knowledge, many people see their personality, or the essence of themselves, as residing in the mind. They view the body as a mere extension of the head, a necessary vehicle for getting the head around. People often don't know much about their bodies and how it works and feel that their bodies are almost separate from themselves. They may be vaguely aware that their bodies are sometimes in pain, that they get tense, or that something may go wrong with the body, but they don't know how to exert control over it. Thinking of the mind and body as separate entities is a mistake, for one is useless without the other. Without the brain, we would have no guiding intelligence to order our activity, and without the body there would be no way of carrying out our activities, of putting our ideas into action. It is true that we are our thoughts, but we are also our bodies and behavior. Finally, even if we understand intellectually that the mind/body is one entity, we may lack the skill to use it efficiently.

Here is an example of how the mind and the body can be at odds with each other. It's an example every Alexander teacher will be familiar with because it happens so often in teaching: A beginning pupil comes for an Alexander lesson and is anxious to learn the technique and to do it correctly. The teacher places a hand on the pupil's neck and asks the pupil not to do anything with his muscles, but just to think what the teacher asks him to think. The teacher instructs the pupil to think of releasing his neck to let his head go forward and up. In response, the pupil pulls his head back in an effort to put his head forward. Even though the student knows he is not supposed to do anything with his muscles, his desire to perform correctly is stronger than his powers of inhibition. In his effort to get it right, he does exactly the wrong thing. His mind/body is out of sync in two ways: He is not able to inhibit unwanted activity, nor is he able to control his desire to get it right. As a result, he uses excess muscle tension. His body and mind are not working together toward a common goal; instead his body is working against his mind. Paradoxically, this state of affairs occurs because the student wants so badly to achieve his goal: doing it right.

Scientific research is currently being conducted as to how the body and the mind affect one another and how the mind might be used to help heal the body. *Anatomy of an Illness* by Norman Cousins, *The Relaxation Response* by Herbert Benson, and *Love, Medicine and Miracles* by Bernard Siegal are all bestselling books that touch on how the two are interconnected. In *Anatomy of an Illness*, Cousins explains how he used laughter and positive thinking to help cure his illness; *The Relaxation Response* puts forward meditation as a medically tested stress reduction technique; and *Love, Medicine and Miracles* suggests that positive thinking and visualization can make a difference in dealing with serious illness. There is some evidence that stress can depress the immune system and leave it more vulnerable to disease, while a fit body and a generally positive attitude toward life help strengthen the immune system. More proof is needed before these theories are widely accepted by the medical profession, but hospitals and private individuals already use some of the techniques outlined in these books. Hospitals and pain clinics also use self-hypnosis, biofeedback, and visualization to help reduce pain and stress.

Perhaps it is wrong to compare the Alexander Technique to these other techniques that claim therapeutic results. Alexander teachers are just that—teachers, rather than therapists. The Alexander Technique is an educational process that teaches pupils how to use themselves with more freedom and ease.

However, there are often beneficial side effects, such as the reduction of stress, tension, and pain. We aren't physicians and are not qualified to present the current scientific evidence of how the mind and body work together. Our evidence is empirical and practical. It is based on what we have observed and experienced in ourselves and in thousands of students. Therefore, we have taken case studies from our files and interviewed people who have studied the Alexander Technique, to see how they have personally experienced the connection between their bodies and minds.

As teachers, we work with people every day and ask them to think certain things in order to bring about changes in their bodies. Our purpose is to promote freedom, ease, and openness in the body so that the muscles and joints can move with top efficiency. Unlike some teachers, we do not ask our students to think of their bodies as balloons filled with helium, or to imagine the tension draining out of their bodies like water down a sink drain—in other words, we do not work with what is usually known as visualization. An Alexander teacher is interested in getting the basic anatomical structure of the human body, the bones and the muscles, and the nervous system which conducts messages from the brain to the muscles, to work together. Alexander teachers use their hands to show their students where the major joints are. In addition, they often use muscle charts and skeletons to familiarize their students with their body structure and show how it is designed to function. We then ask students to take this knowledge and apply it directly to their body structure. Whatever verbal information is given to the student is usually directly related to how the body is put together, how it works, and how to influence it through thinking.

At first the mind/body connection may seem almost magical to our students, but to Alexander teachers it is simply a fact. We can ask certain changes to take place in our own bodies and we know that they will take place because we have had the experience ourselves over and over again. If an Alexander teacher asks her neck to release, a message is sent from her brain through the nervous system to her muscle, and the muscle releases the excess tension. We have also seen these changes take place in thousands of students. The changes in nerve and muscle activity brought about by thought can be measured by electromyographic (EMG) equipment. Studies have been done using this equipment that have shown the decrease in muscle tension and the spinal lengthening that result from using the Alexander Technique.* The release through thought process is not familiar to the new student; therefore, it can seem mysterious. But as students become more adept at the process of sending mental messages to their bodies, the process becomes less surprising and can be counted upon to make changes.

As with learning any skill, this takes practice. You cannot sit down at your first piano lesson and play Mozart—you learn simple scales, then more complex exercises, simple tunes, and then more complex melodies. It is the same with the Alexander Technique. First you learn to inhibit excess tension in the body and direct the body to do something else. Your body obeys the instructions as best it can at that point in time. As you continue to instruct yourself in this way, the process becomes easier and easier. You reach new levels of awareness, and your sensory feedback mechanism becomes more sensitive to subtler messages.

When first studying the Alexander Technique, you will have to stop and inhibit often. You will find yourself in awkward positions without really knowing how you got there—for example, you may suddenly

* Jones, F. P. *Body Awareness in Action: A Study of the Alexander Technique*. New York: Schocken Books, 1979.

find that you are slumped in front of the television set or have hunched over a sink to wash your hands. You then pause and inhibit, send the directions to help yourself out of the situation, and continue the activity with improved body use. Your mind is saying to your body, in effect, "Hey, wait a minute, what are you doing? You're all in a knot." As you continue to work with the Alexander Technique, your sensory mechanism will become more and more sensitive. Eventually your body will let you know quite quickly when you could be using yourself more efficiently, and the changes will become more subtle. For example, you may look fine and be fairly upright but still feel a heaviness in your body. In this case the body will talk to the mind by sending messages of pain or discomfort to the brain. Once your mind is alerted by your sensory mechanism, you can say to yourself, "I'm feeling sort of heavy and awkward; I guess I'm not using myself very well. I'd better think my directions." As you can see, sometimes the body talks to the mind and sometimes the mind talks to the body.

When teaching small groups we use an exercise that works very well to show how the mind affects the body. The students take partners, and one partner sits in a chair while the other stands facing his partner. The sitting partners are instructed to think of themselves as weighing a ton, and the standing partners are instructed to get the others out of their chairs any way they can without hurting themselves or their partners. Usually laughter abounds as the standing partners try to heave immobile bodies out of chairs. It doesn't matter how light the sitter is—she can be a slim girl of one hundred pounds, but she can make herself very heavy through thinking. We then ask the seated partners to think the Alexander directions, which promote freedom and lightness in the body; the sitter is then easily guided out of the chair. Changing the thought process changes how the body is balanced, and when it is balanced it moves very easily.

One of the questions we asked our students in our interviews for this book was how they felt their bodies and minds were connected. We have summarized their answers here because they explain the connection in a direct and practical way.

Many students talked about how the mind, body, and emotions work as a coordinated unit. They have discovered that as their body and mind begin to work more smoothly together, their outlook changes and they become more optimistic and open. One student said, "I can't think my directions and be depressed at the same time. I think they are incompatible." Another student agreed and added, "The freedom and changes that happen in my musculature have an effect on my thinking. After I have a lesson it seems to loosen something in my psyche, and I have new insights about myself. I understand more about the way I behave."

The first question we asked about the mind/ body was "Do you think the mind and the body are connected?" Not one student questioned the concept or even hesitated before answering. Many answered quickly and spontaneously like Ben: "Absolutely! Unquestionably! The mind and the body work in tandem!" He went on to say:

> I walk a lot delivering my artwork; I need the exercise. If I'm crunching down, my body will tell me to stop it and then I direct. In the beginning, I repeated the directions to myself and I didn't feel much happening. I didn't get much feedback from my body. Now my sensory mechanism tells me when I'm tensing much more often, but my body responds much more quickly when I think the

directions. The mind and body must be connected or they wouldn't be talking to each other!

Many students reported that they couldn't even think of the body and the mind separately any more. Helena said, "They are two aspects of the same thing. Sometimes one speaks louder than the other and so you listen to that one. I get messages from my mind about my body, and messages from my body about my mind." She described the feeling as getting messages from two different places, but from the same source. She said that when she learns something about herself during her Alexander lessons, something happens in her body that quickly registers in her mind as being important: "It's almost as though the information magically flashes up onto a screen in my head and I will think, 'Aha! This is what I've been doing wrong with my body all these years.'" Helena, like Ben, experiences a dialogue between two aspects of herself.

John told us what happens to him when his mind and body don't work together: "Before I had Alexander lessons my body and my mind seemed to work at two different rhythms. My mind worked very quickly, racing ahead of me, and my body got left behind. It was like I was a car and I put myself in neutral and let the motor run, so my mind was racing away but I wasn't getting anywhere." The technique helped John get out of that mode, to think at a speed that is more in tune with his natural body speed—he calls it "body time": "When I can work in body time I feel coordinated. Things that used to bother me don't, and I feel at peace with myself. I sense a dialogue between body and mind, and I have fun exploring everyday movements." Becoming more aware of, and having more control over, his thinking process, he is able to use his imagination in a different way: "I love watching sports. There are many types of sports that I could never do, but I have an appreciation of them because with my mind I can put myself in the athlete's body and feel what they're doing, and I have a real sense of satisfaction from that."

Emily, a teacher, said:

I don't think anyone really knows all the scientific details of how the mind and the body work together, but it is clear to me that they do. The state of my body affects the way I think. It also affects the way I feel, my self-image, and my belief systems. The opposite is also true—the state of mind affects my body. My belief systems and my self-image affect how I see my mind and my body, so they are all intricately interconnected and inseparable. I know that if I inhibit and direct, this helps to free everything—my mind, my body, my emotions—and helps with my self-image.

One after another, students commented on how the mind and body were intertwined and said what a relief it was to have a tool that gave them control over themselves. One student, Emilia, said, "My reaction to stress is to tighten up; that's my learned behavior. But now when I catch myself tensing in my neck and shoulders I can do something about it. I've learned that I do have control through my thinking; the ability to allow my muscles to release. I can think my way into doing this. I am training myself to react to stress in new ways through the Alexander Technique." Emilia is using her mind to take a moment to inhibit, to allow her body to choose a different response to a stressful situation.

Another student, Jim, pointed out that we have the ability to pay attention to any part of our body, and with practice, the whole body at the same time: "There is an intelligence through the whole body. Everything will wake up if you help all the parts connect to the whole. It's like every cell has a mind or intelligence, and by using the brain to relate to a certain body part, you can engage that part of the body and make it become active and conscious."

Jane's powers of observation have sharpened considerably since she began studying the technique. She feels that the way people move and the way they think are directly connected: "The lack of cohesiveness in our thinking is betrayed by jerky body movements, a frenetic physical state, and unrestfulness in the eyes." She went on to say, "The question is—are you a functioning unity or a nonfunctioning unity?" Her husband, Kevin, agrees that the mind and body work together whether we are aware of it or not: "They always work together. We have the choice to have them work together on a more highly skilled awareness level or not. Having a discipline that teaches you to be aware of yourself in movement and activities and that gives you a choice of behavior responses helps the two work together more efficiently and easefully."

Before taking Alexander lessons David didn't· want to know anything about anatomy or how the body worked. Thoughts of that type made him very uneasy. He felt that anything that was important was happening in his head. He almost wished he didn't have a body. As he said: "I was in denial about my body. I never took responsibility for my body. I think that's a classic problem. My body was very tight and tense and I thought my body would change if I did repetitive body building exercises—in other words, if I just moved my body around without any thought. I realized that I was afraid of my body in a way, afraid that it wouldn't do what I wanted it to. I thought of it as totally disconnected from my thinking process. I also despised it in a way." In David's case it took a long time, but he was able to stop hating his body. It slowly became less and less tense and, from being rigid and in pain, grew to move fluidly and with grace.

Sue attempted to describe what she feels like when her body and mind work together: "I wish I could describe the feeling—there's a wholeness, a complete feeling and I am utterly connected. My brain is connected to my feet and everything in between. When I am not connected I feel like they fight each other." Kitty experiences something similar: "After a lesson I feel buzzy and very alive. I see myself more as an energy system, less like meat and bones that I have to haul around town."

Many students said that one of the most important things they learned from the Alexander Technique was that they could exert more control over their bodies. Jeremy said that he was aware that his posture was bad and it caused him physical discomfort. He thought he could control it through exercise: "I swim a couple of miles a day, and I thought that it would help my bad posture, but actually it didn't do anything to help my body misuse. Then I thought that I would have to do a vigorous exercise program in order to correct the problem. Luckily I didn't have time to fit it into my schedule." What he meant by *luckily* was that his body use was so bad, he is now convinced he would have hurt himself doing the exercises. After studying the technique, he was able to start an exercise program with good body use: "It was a revelation to me that putting yourself into a certain state of mind you can change your body. It's a mental discipline. First I had to learn that I had to change my attitude—unlearn old attitudes and learn a new frame of mind. It wasn't always easy. It was a process; it gets deeper and deeper. Sometimes I catch myself falling into old habits, but I can get myself out of it now. My workouts are better—they are quicker and more efficient—and I breathe more deeply." Alphonse realized that his old attitude about exercise—pushing hard for results—was actually detrimental to his workout. He found that when he could release his body, stay focused on which parts should be working, and make sure that he didn't hold his breath, his workouts went much better.

Another student, Clare, agreed that the first thing that needs to change is attitude if the mind/body is to work more easily: "It annoys me when people call the Alexander Technique 'body work.' They don't seem to understand, even if they are extremely intelligent and very well educated people, that their own thinking process creates difficulties. You asked me, 'How are we united?' My response is, 'How are we not united?' Even when we are most malcoordinated, the body and the mind work together. They work badly together then, but one still affects the other."

Two students, Chuck and Carrie, described how the mental stress that they placed on themselves led to physical manifestations. Chuck told us, "I used to grip my teeth so tightly when I slept that they would hurt like hell when I woke up. I held in my emotions, so I held in my body." For Carrie, the mind/body connection is crystal clear: "When I am tense emotionally, my deep back muscles tighten. If I'm very, very tense emotionally, then my back goes out. I get emotionally tense when I hold back my feelings and don't let other people know that I am upset. As long as I express my feelings, my back doesn't go out." Several students said that by freeing their bodies of excess tension through studying the technique, they had sped up their psychotherapy.

Kevin, a student of the Alexander Technique and a practicing psychotherapist, explained, "If the mind thinks we are a certain way, the body responds to that thought, and we become the way we use our bodies. Our beliefs have a very strong influence on our bodies. If I believe I am a victim of circumstances, I will assume a posture that will agree with that attitude, which will reinforce the belief. Attitudes have a physical expression; you can walk down the streets of our cities and towns and see that without trying very hard. It's a universal body language."

Jessica had an experience that not all students have. When her body was worked on and released, it seemed to trigger memories from her past, emotional traumas that she had experienced but not expressed her response to at the time: "I got a lot of flashbacks as my body released and changed, insights into past responses. I understood why I behaved in certain ways in the past. It wasn't a process of reflecting carefully, but of memories coming to the surface." The psychologist Wilheim Reich, who named the phenomenon "body armoring," believed that if people, especially children, experienced an emotional trauma and did not express their feelings at the time (sometimes because they were not able to under the circumstances), the trauma would somehow be trapped in the muscles. Later on, when the muscles were freed in a nurturing environment, this signaled the brain that the trauma was ready to be processed.

A student named Katy shared the story of how she began taking lessons. She had just graduated from college and moved to New York and her mother gave her a series of Alexander lessons as a gift. Katy was a struggling dancer and was feeling depressed: "My Alexander teacher was very supportive when I was going through a lot of emotional trauma. I cried in a few lessons and felt that was OK. The lessons were a unique and moving experience for me. The process seemed mysterious and wonderful. Part of me was awake and aware of what was going on, and another part was asleep, unconscious and unaware, but I knew

part of me was asleep." Katy said that her body phys-
icalized the emotional stress and tension she felt.
When her physical tensions were eased, her emotional
state improved. She learned that she could have almost
a third eye that was aware of what was happening in
her mind, body, and emotions. It gave her perspective
and allowed her conscious choice about her behavior.

If your body is not working efficiently, your
body and mind can feel at odds, or you may even be
aware of one and not the other. But whether you are
well balanced or not, your body and the mind work in
tandem, and you can choose to have them work together in better alignment and closer harmony. By
working with the Alexander concepts of inhibition and
direction, you can become clearer in your thinking and
more fluid and at ease in your body. This in turn will
enhance your functioning and enjoyment in daily activities.

Self-Image and
Psychological Factors ℘

An Alexander teacher is not a psychotherapist, but since the Alexander Technique involves the mind and the body, the teacher sometimes has to deal with students' self-images, self-concepts, or habitual ways of thinking about themselves. The teacher's job is to show you how to inhibit habitual reactions to stimuli so that you leave yourself open to choose your reaction. You choose whether or not you wish to use the Alexander principles to improve your body mechanics and movement, and you also choose whether you wish to integrate the Alexander principles more fully into your life. If you choose to do so, the moment of inhibition becomes not just a moment to stop poor physical use, but also a moment to consider how you wish to react on every level, including the mental and emotional.

Unfortunately, many of us have a low opinion of ourselves. Your self-image may be a hodgepodge of beliefs that are left over from:

- what family, friends, colleagues,

acquaintances, and enemies have said about
you
- what society says about your race, creed,
  income bracket, place of origin, and
  education
- what you have thought about yourself

Our self-images have often been with us since
early childhood, and it is difficult for us to alter them
even if our circumstances have altered. If you were a
chubby little girl and are now a slender, attractive
woman, you may still hold the idea in your head that
you are too heavy. If you were unpopular as a young
boy, even though you are now a popular, successful
man, you may still picture yourself as a "nerd."
One aspect of self-image is personal appearance. One student told us that through the Alexander
Technique she learned to accept what she looked like:
"My self-image had always been very poor. I would
look at myself in the mirror and turn away from it
immediately. I couldn't accept how I looked. I lacked
confidence in my abilities; I didn't give myself credit
for what I could do. I can look at myself now and not
groan." Another student said, "I used to exercise and
exercise and exercise. I was a fanatic. The technique
helped me to realize that I was a certain body type, I
couldn't change my height, I couldn't change the size
of my bones—and even though I was not petite, I
wasn't fat. I relaxed. I exercised less and enjoyed it
more. I'm so grateful that I can now like myself." Yet
another student said:

Before, if I ever caught a glimpse of myself in
a mirror or store window, I felt really
uncomfortable and unattractive. Now if I see
myself sometimes I feel fine about what I see.

But if I'm having a hard day and I feel very tired or down about something and I see myself, I might start to get the old feeling of not liking what I see. But I can improve it on the spot by inhibiting and directing. If I inhibit tension I feel better about myself; I don't feel as awkward. My mother has noticed these changes. She loved seeing me dress up for my job interviews recently because I no longer have my defensive posture; now I'm much more open to the world. I can let myself get dolled up and present myself to the world and feel good about it. This attitude reflects itself in my body. It's amazing, but it's also fun. A very different self is coming through.

An attractive young woman with a good body that was in perfect proportion came into her Alexander teacher's office one day quite upset. It was the beginning of the summer and she was convinced that she would look awful in a bathing suit, "I have no shoulders and I'm going to look like a pear!" she said. Her teacher told her, "It's all in your mind. Your self-image is that you are pear-shaped and that's not accurate. Look in the mirror." The student looked in the mirror and still thought she looked like a pear. The teacher could see that the woman's body was perfectly proportioned, but there was excess tension in her shoulders. The teacher and student spent the whole lesson working on her shoulders. At the end of the lesson the tension had released and her shoulders widened. She later said, "After that lesson, not only did my shoulders look wonderful, a fundamental change had happened and I began to think of myself differently. My self-image changed. I realized that my teacher was right, that I had been convinced that I was a certain shape and I made myself become that shape by squeezing my shoulders tightly together. When I changed the mental picture in my head, my body was able to relax, my shoulders expanded, and I actually took the next size bigger in a blouse." When people have a body shape in their minds that they think is theirs, they make their bodies conform to it. They literally contort themselves. The face, the neck, the lower back, or the whole body can tighten and become misshapen. With the release of tension comes an improvement in your self-image, a type of positive reinforcement.

One woman felt that the technique was responsible for her staying youthful looking:

I went to my high school's twentieth reunion and I was nominated as the person who had changed the least in physical appearance. I attribute it to the fact that my posture hasn't changed in twenty years and to my youthful way of moving. Both of these I attribute to the Alexander Technique. Everyone else's posture was much worse and showed their age. I didn't show my age. I've had numerous people come up to me and say, "Your posture's incredible, what kind of exercise do you do?" I just had a baby and people couldn't believe I was thirty-nine. People think I am up to ten years younger than I really am.

Some people think that with age comes automatic postural disintegration; this does not have to be true. We both know men and women who are in their sixties, seventies, and even their eighties who look wonderful and have not lost their ability to use their bodies well. If you have no medical conditions that restrict movement or impair good posture, such as arthritis or osteoporosis, there is no reason why you shouldn't use your body well until the end of your life.

Students report that after studying the technique they look longer and leaner, their faces relax and look more attractive, their physical movement becomes more graceful, and they develop a type of "presence" or poise that makes them feel more confident and self-assured. One said, "I was the classic klutz. I bumped into walls, I tripped over rugs and fell off of curbs. Now I have something I never thought I would —poise. I feel calm inside and I have awareness and control of what my body is doing." Another student said, "Before I took lessons in the Alexander Technique I felt very insecure. I didn't have much self-confidence. My approach to life was to work hard and exert a lot of effort. I did too much when I was trying to accomplish things. As a result I limited myself. I didn't have as much flexibility and freedom as I could have. I was very self-conscious about my body and much more afraid of dealing with emotional issues before studying the Alexander Technique." Another said, "I feel much less caught off guard by the demands of living, less taken by surprise when I have to make a spur-of-the-moment decision. I can say no when I have to—I never could before. I feel emotionally more in control."

Many students report a lessening of both physical and mental tension, pressure that they placed on themselves. This reduction of tension makes them feel lighter in their bodies, and also in their spirits. As one student put it:

> I am now open to doing things that would not have fit into my self-concept before. Things feel possible. My concept of myself used to be much more rigid, like "Yes, I do this, but no, I don't do that." New things used to

intimidate me. Now I feel like I can try whatever I want, and the technique gives me a way to take it slowly and go step by step. I'm not so hung up on whether I will be good at it or whether I fail, but just deal with things in the moment. That applies to social situations and the way I relate to people too. I love to try new things. I even took up the conga drum!

People often drive themselves so hard they don't allow themselves adequate rest and time off from thinking about work and their problems. Their minds are always running. The Alexander Technique can give them the physical experience of release in their bodies so that they realize they can leave their bodies and minds free when they choose to: "Sometimes I work too hard and I get very stressed out. Then my body really takes a beating. It feeds on itself and I can tell my body is getting weaker, almost like it's ill. I can now get myself feeling relaxed. I can allow myself moments of peace and repose, something I've not felt before."

The technique can be a support system in a time of unusual stress and tension. The directions keep you from sinking physically at a time when you need your maximum amount of energy. An Alexander teacher we know shared a story with us from her own life:

> I was under a lot of pressure because of a serious illness in my family. I was in charge of taking care of my step-mother's needs, which was really a full-time job. In addition I was doing my regular private teaching. I was anticipating starting to work in the training class [with students who are training to be Alexander teachers] in the next month and I

was very apprehensive about taking on the additional work. I thought that the extra hours of work combined with the emotional strain would be too much for me. It was fine. It was amazing, because even though the work in the training class took many hours and was extremely demanding, it stimulated me rather than making my problems worse. It lightened my burden because the work is so restorative.

Many students have felt that their physical restrictions reflected a larger restriction in themselves. One student put it most clearly when he said, "The discomfort, difficulty, and unreliability that I had continually experienced in physical activity led to a very negative self-image about my body and who I was. This severely restricted my emotional life and my interpersonal relationships." Another said:

The Alexander Technique provided an enormous opening for me to begin to deal with my emotional habits. My body was very tight, and by releasing it, I became more open to my total being, which had a lot of emotional tensions. My emotional issues were locked into my body. That's one reason my body was so rigid. I certainly didn't come out of the womb that way! By the time I got to my late teens I became really aware of these tensions; I was very identified with them; that was just who I was. But I also knew at some level that it wasn't normal to be that tied up. In my lessons I began to unwind the muscle tensions. Then I became more aware of my emotional habits and was able to begin to change what I didn't like in myself. Now I can ask myself, "Why am I behaving this way?," explore how I got to have the habit, and change it.

Just as we all have physical habits, we have emotional habits as well, ways of behaving in situations that are habitual. But with the use of the Alexander Technique we can learn to change them. Through the use of inhibition we can say no to old emotional habits we want to change. "Things that used to make me crazy don't any more," explained one of our students. "The technique makes me feel good. I don't get in a circular grind of negativity that feeds on itself. I catch myself in negative emotions and I can stop it if I want to. I feel much better and healthier."

Another student described how a physical experience that he had in a lesson—standing on his feet in a different way—led him to a different emotional sense of himself: "It was startling when I realized that I could really stand on my own two feet—this had a lot of psychological implications. It meant that I could really be balanced over my feet and not be collapsed and leaning forward. It was like I was saying, 'I can take responsibility for myself and be on my feet and meet the world.' I was standing up on my own, practically for the first time in my life."

Occasionally the changes that take place physically and emotionally will bring up feelings of anxiety:

My self-image was that everything I needed was in my head, that my life was taking place mainly in my head. I was afraid of my body and of moving it, and that shut my body down. I needed to have my fear worked on in an indirect way. The Alexander Technique provided that way. At the end of a lesson I was much taller and longer, almost aristocratic looking. My teacher would sometimes ask me, "What's wrong with looking like this?" The questions made me anxious. I somehow didn't feel worthy of looking that way. Gradually my self-image changed and I am comfortable with it now. I can look tall and elegant and not be apologetic for how I look.

Another student made a similar point in a different way:

I had terrible pain in my right ear when I was a little girl because of an illness. Many years later I still unconsciously tilted my head to the right, which was a habitual-use pattern. I had a very firm sense of myself as being in that posture and attitude. In one of my lessons my teacher moved my head to center it, and I felt strongly that I was tilting to the left. When the teacher told me to look in the mirror to check it out, I looked and saw that my head was indeed straight. I had a moment of panic, a mini identity crisis. Part of who I was was not what I thought it was. Your identity is your belief about what you know to be true, and a belief about myself had been incorrect. It was hard to accept at first.

This woman was able to look in the mirror and see that her alignment was improved after working with her teacher. But even though she could see that she looked better and understood that improved body use would improve her functioning, she was afraid of giving up a part of herself, however "negative." This process of giving up old habits is a part of changing. Although change is wonderful and exciting, there can be moments of doubt and uncertainty as you give up what is familiar.

One woman we spoke to said, "I was having back problems and I blamed myself. I didn't know why it was happening, so I thought there was something wrong with me, almost like I was handicapped." Through her work on the technique she was gradually able to change her view of herself as she learned how to control the muscle spasm in her back. She is now in much less pain. She can also usually feel when a back spasm is coming on and, by inhibiting and directing, can avoid it. Even if she can't predict a spasm, she has a tool she can use to make herself feel better relatively quickly. She says, "I feel like less of a victim, less passive. Now I am no longer so afraid of my back, and I no longer think I am a bad person for having a back that is somewhat unstable. I am now a participant in life."

The most striking answer anyone gave us to the question, "Has the Alexander Technique had an effect on your self-image?" was "I didn't have a self-image before I studied the technique." Before studying the Alexander Technique, this student didn't have positive feelings of self-worth, but he didn't know that he felt that way. With the Alexander Technique he experienced a gradual change in his feelings about himself as he gave up his old patterns of behavior.

The Alexander Technique will affect every level of ourselves—physical, mental, and emotional—if we allow it. If we choose, we can use the technique to bring about significant physical improvements and nothing more. But if we wish to explore our full potential, we must be aware of how we react and behave, question what we want to change, and use the tools of inhibition and direction to change what we want to change. After working with these tools over a period of time, we won't have to consider each level whenever we stop to inhibit; the inhibition of mental, emotional, and physical habits will synergize into a whole, and when we inhibit, we will inhibit on all of these levels.

What Happens in Alexander Lessons ⤸

Most people take Alexander lessons for a specific purpose. A doctor, chiropractor, or physical therapist may refer a patient for Alexander lessons because they feel the patient has poor posture, pain, or stress symptoms that may be reduced by a course of Alexander lessons. Others may hear about the Alexander Technique through friends or read about it and want to learn more. Many students don't have medical conditions—they decide they want to learn how to move better, look better, improve their self-image, or feel less tense. Some are referred by acting, dancing, or singing teachers who feel the technique can help their students improve the use of their voice and body in performance and in everyday life.

To help you understand more about what actually happens in Alexander lessons and how the process of learning it works, we have included many of the questions that new students ask us:

How many lessons should I take and how often?

The number of lessons you need depends on you, what you want to work on, and what your objectives are. Alexander had his students come for a "course of lessons"—five times a week for six weeks, for a total of thirty lessons. Major changes could be made in this relatively short period of time. Since the lessons were so close together, there was little time for the body to fall back into old habits, and it was possible for each lesson to build on the next in a very concrete way. After thirty lessons, some students continued to take lessons once a week for as long as the lessons were helpful to them; others stopped and came back periodically for a course of refresher lessons. However, we are living in a time when most people no longer have the time or financial resources to study under such ideal circumstances.

Today most students take a lesson once or twice a week, depending on their circumstances. It is possible to make major changes studying at this frequency, but of course it takes longer than six weeks. Students who have the time should ideally take three lessons a week for two weeks, then two lessons a week for three weeks, followed by lessons once a week. This method of timing the lessons allows the student to get a strong dose of the technique in a short period of time, and keeps the body from falling too far back into its old habits. After the first ten lessons the student will understand the basic Alexander concepts and will be able to remind himself of them between lessons. He is then ready to have lessons once a week.

Some people take Alexander lessons for a specific reason. You may have a minor tension problem, for instance. Once you learn how to use your body in a more effective way, you can use your newfound awareness to help yourself unwind when you find yourself tensing. Alexander teachers still suggest a course of thirty lessons once or twice weekly to achieve this goal. But if you have severe back problems, tension, and stress difficulties, or if your habits of movement are more ingrained, you may choose to come for more than thirty lessons. Very few teachers require that a student come for a required number of lessons. We suggest to our students that they come as long as they feel the lessons are helpful to them. The Alexander Technique is an acquired skill, and like any other skill it takes time to learn. If you choose to learn to play the piano or speak French, for example, you'll need some time to become proficient; in addition, you can learn the skill at a simple and basic level, or you can become expert, depending on your desire. It is the same with the Alexander Technique.

How long are the lessons?

Alexander lessons are generally thirty or forty-five minutes long, depending on the teacher's preference. Lessons that are any longer than this don't seem to be productive. Learning the technique requires you to focus on yourself and your habits quite intently and there seems to be a point of diminishing returns.

How much do lessons cost?

Lessons can cost anywhere between thirty and seventy dollars per session, depending on what part of the country you are in and who you are studying with.

Where do Alexander teachers teach?

Most teachers work in private offices or in their homes. A few teachers are connected with hospital pain clinics or physical therapy and teach in those settings.

Is the Alexander Technique covered by insurance companies?

This depends on the insurance company. Unfortunately, many do not cover it. The reason may be that Alexander teachers are not licensed by the state the way physical therapists are. Another reason may be that the technique is primarily educational in nature, though it has many therapeutic benefits. Some insurance companies will reimburse you for your lessons; ask your company before you sign up for your first lesson.

If you are referred by a physician for a specific ailment, get a prescription for lessons and have the doctor state the diagnosis. Make copies of the prescription and send one each time you send a form to your insurance company. The company may or may not reimburse you. Perhaps more companies will recognize the technique as a valuable tool in the future.

What happens in the first Alexander lesson?

It depends on what your teacher feels is necessary for you. Each teacher's style is slightly different, and certainly each student's needs are different; these factors will dictate what course the teacher takes. There is no disrobing or physical examination. You may wear your regular clothes as long as they are not tight and restrictive, or you may be more comfortable wearing exercise clothing that allows for free movement of the body. The teachers use their hands to guide you into a new experience of your body. They may begin by asking you some questions such as:

- Have you had Alexander lessons in the past?
- Who referred you for lessons and why?
- If you have not been referred, why have you decided to have lessons?
- Do you suffer from any conditions such as neck or back pain or sciatica or any physical injuries? If so, have you consulted your physician about it?
- Do you suffer from pain?

- Have you been in any accidents?
- Do you take part in any sports or physical activity?

The teacher may also ask you what type of job you have to find out if you sit all day, are on your feet all day, or have to lift and carry or stoop over a good part of the time. These questions are not used to "diagnose" you in the way a physician would, but simply to find out what has happened to your body in the past and what is happening to it now in order to choose an approach to teaching you. For example, if you are a dentist and stoop over patients all day, the Alexander teacher might first choose to show you ways of bending that are beneficial to the body, rather than harmful. (But this depends on the teacher's approach. Another teacher might begin in another way for equally good reasons.) Teachers will briefly explain the technique before using their hands to work with you, or they may choose to explain as they are working. They may begin working by guiding you through simple everyday movement activities such as getting in and out of a chair and walking, or they may begin working with you as you lie on a table.

Alexander teachers' hands are unforceful; they guide you gently and never push you beyond where you can go. They point out where you can release excess tension and show you how to coordinate your body so that it works together smoothly as a whole. You may feel a dramatic difference in your body, or you may not feel much at first, but instead get a sense of what the technique is about. Sometimes habits are so strong that it takes a while for subtle messages to get through to the kinesthetic sense.

At the end of the lesson the teacher may recommend an Alexander book for you to read (we hope it's this one!) or give you articles to help explain the technique to you. We recommend that you take two or three lessons before you decide whether or not you would like to study. You won't understand everything about the technique, but you will have a general sense about whether you like it and the teacher. If you like both you can continue. If for some reason you don't feel comfortable with one teacher, try others until you find one you feel you can work with. The teacher and student work closely together, so it is important that you feel comfortable together.

What happens in the lessons that follow the first?

There is no set system that every teacher follows; everything the teacher does is custom designed for the student. There are ways of moving, bending, and reaching that all teach repeatedly, but when these movements are introduced, how they are introduced, how they are explained, and how they lead into the next point to be learned is completely at the teacher's discretion.

Generally, teachers work with the student both in movement and lying down at each lesson. Having said that, there may be times when the teacher chooses to work solely with the student lying down or solely with the student in movement because there is something specific to be worked on. The movement work is very practical and helps you to learn how to apply the Alexander principles to everyday life: walking, sitting, standing, reaching, bending, and so forth. The teacher has many ways of showing you how you may be inefficient in these activities and how to go about changing yourself. The lying down work is helpful since you don't have to concern yourself with gravity; you can take more chances letting go of excess tension when you don't have to worry about keeping yourself upright. The teacher circles the table, working with all parts of your body. Although the teacher's hands will be placed on many different parts of your body, the objective is always to help you release your neck so that your head can release forward and up so that your torso can release into its full length and width.

At some point the teacher may decide to help apply the Alexander principles to daily activities. Often this will happen spontaneously. For instance, a student may be carrying a heavy bag one day and say, "Oh, I'm having such trouble carrying this around." The teacher may then suggest that they work on how to carry heavy bags. The teacher may suggest applying the Alexander principles to everyday activities, or the student may ask to work on something specific. For example, musicians may want to bring their instruments so that the teacher can see what they are doing as they play. Work with the teacher can help to relieve harmful tension habits and often will indirectly help their playing. The reduction of tension will have an effect on how much effort they use when playing and, more importantly, will have an effect on the whole attitude they bring to their practicing, playing, and approach to music. Most musicians have been trained in such a way that when they play a wrong note they play the passage over and over again until they get it right. Unfortunately, what often happens is that they get tenser and tenser as they work with it. The Alexander teacher can teach musicians how to leave the body free as they practice a difficult passage so that they are more likely to get it right, and if they are unable to get it right at the moment, to leave it and go on to something else. Later they can return to the passage fresh to try again. Freeing the body can even improve the quality of the sound!

The teacher's job is to show the student how to inhibit the habitual reaction to a stimulus and then choose whatever course of action the student wants to take. Students are then able to help themselves when they find themselves tense, stressed, fatigued, or in a difficult life situation.

What are group classes like?

Although the Alexander Technique has traditionally been taught one-on-one, group classes are now available. Group classes cannot provide the intense personal attention private lessons can, but they can be useful in some circumstances. Some Alexander teachers teach introductory group workshops, which are helpful for people who would like to get a taste of the technique before they invest in private lessons. Group lessons are also helpful because in a group you can watch changes happen in other people. Group classes can be helpful as an adjunct to private lessons for performing artists, giving them the opportunity to perform in front of others while working on the Alexander principles.

Obviously, group classes are more economical then private lessons, but private lessons are always preferable to group classes. You must remember that the hands-on help is the most important part of the lesson; in a group class each student receives only a few minutes of individual attention. In a group class the teacher doesn't have time to deal with the specific needs of the individual student.

How does the teacher know when I am releasing my muscles?

Alexander teachers have been highly trained and are sensitive to very subtle releases in the body. Since the teacher's body and hands are very free, they are able to feel things that the average person cannot. Some of the releases that the teacher feels will be below the sense register of the student; in other words, they will be so small that the student can't feel them (although the student learns to feel more and more). The Alexander teacher never forces a change upon a student but asks the student to think the directions so that messages are sent from the student's brain through the nervous system to the muscles. Once the teacher feels a release, he or she can encourage the student to go further in that direction: It is a dialogue between the teacher and student. Although students may sometimes feel that the teacher is "lifting them up," it is only because the student has consented to change and give up some tension that the release can occur at all.

Why won't the teacher let me close my eyes when I am lying on the table? It helps me relax.

The main purpose is not to relax but to *release* the body in specific directions to bring about a coordinated whole. Your eyes should stay open so you don't lose touch with what's happening. With your eyes open, the teacher can check to make sure that isn't happening. Glazed eyes indicate that the body is stiffening. The teacher's goal is to show you how to apply the technique to life, so you need to be aware of what's happening inside your body, but also what is happening in the environment around you.

Will the Alexander teacher give me exercises to practice?

No. There are no exercises in the Alexander Technique. Learning the technique means learning how to inhibit and direct. You may then apply those concepts to anything you do. The one exception to this may be if you have a physical problem such as back pain or sciatica; the teacher may suggest some very simple things for you to do in between lessons to ease up your body. If you are in pain of any kind we suggest that you read *Back Trouble* by Deborah Caplan, who is a physical therapist and Alexander teacher. Her book has physical therapy exercises that she has adapted with her Alexander knowledge to help people who are in pain.

How can I work on myself in between Alexander lessons?

After the first few lessons there isn't too much that you can do for yourself. The technique will be new to you and it takes a while to understand what the teacher is asking of you. But there are three things you can do for yourself right from the beginning. The first is to begin to observe yourself in everyday life, to see what your habits of movement are. The most important thing to notice is what you are doing with your neck and head. What happens to them when you brush your teeth, open doors, pick up the telephone, walk down the street? You will probably discover that you are tightening your neck and pulling your head back and down much more often than you were aware of. At first you won't be able to do much about it, but you have to become aware of your habits before you can inhibit them effectively on your own. Later on you will be able to stop the pull back and down.

Secondly, you can begin to observe the people around you to see what they are doing. Watch people on the street, in restaurants, in shopping centers, and see what they are doing with their bodies. You will see them do the most amazing things! You will clearly see other people pulling their necks forward, pulling their heads back and down, and generally twisting and contorting their bodies. It is easier to see poor movement and body use on others than it is on yourself; learning from them will help you learn things about your own body use. Also, make a point to watch people who use themselves very well—you can watch films of Fred Astaire, Arthur Rubenstein, Dame Margot Fonteyn, and Baryshnikov or watch some of the top athletes and dancers. Watching beautiful and easeful movement will help you understand what you are aiming at. You may also want to cut out photographs of good and poor body use from the newspaper, as they will sharpen your eye. As time goes on, your eye will become more acute and accurate.

The third thing you can do for yourself right away is to lie down on a firm surface like an exercise mat or carpeted floor and think your Alexander directions. Unless you are in severe pain, it's better to do this on the floor than on a bed, which you will tend to sink into. A firmer surface gives you more sensory feedback about what you are doing with your body; it will tell you when you are tightening, for example. Lie on your back with books under your head for support (so that your head doesn't pull back and down), with your knees bent and your feet flat on the floor. (Your knees should be bent so that your lower back doesn't arch unduly.) Think your Alexander directions for ten to twenty minutes while lying down. This will reinforce the work you are doing with your teacher, help your body become more familiar with the directions, and help free your body. You should do it as often as possible, preferably several times a week.

When you are more advanced in the technique, you will be able to apply inhibition and direction to whatever you do during the day. You needn't put special time aside to "practice Alexander." You simply apply it when the activity presents itself. You certainly can't think about the technique twenty-four hours a day, but you can remind yourself to keep from falling into old habit patterns. Learning takes place on both the conscious and unconscious level, and some learning will take place through muscle memory. So the more you think of Alexander on the conscious level, the more likely you'll continue using it when you're not thinking about it.

Is the technique automatic, or do I have to think about it between lessons?

You would probably get something out of your lessons even if you had a lesson and then forgot about the technique until your next lesson. But the more you think about the technique outside of your lessons, the more you will progress, and the quicker your progress will be. Remember, the main way to learn the Alexander Technique is through your conscious control—in other words, through using your mental capacities to direct your activity.

Why is it that I am able to release my muscles well in my lessons but find it more difficult when I am on my own?

It is always easier when a teacher is there to help you. The teacher is an outside, objective guide who can see things about you more easily than you can simply by being separate from you. When you release, the teacher's hand can always take you further and show you that you can free yourself even more than you thought possible. It is your job to apply what you learn to your life as best you can. Habits are very ingrained and take time to change. It is impossible to predict how long it will take to change a habit. You have to stay with the process and be as patient with yourself as you can. Remind yourself where you started and you will see how far you've come.

Can I study the Alexander Technique if I am in severe pain or if I am handicapped?

Yes. There are a few people who are so overwhelmed by pain that any type of hands-on instruction or therapy, no matter how subtle and gentle, is too much for them, but the Alexander Technique is generally excellent for helping to relieve pain. People who suffer from pain usually feel much better after their lessons.

You may remember from Judith's story that she suffered from polio. Handicapped people can not only study the technique but can go on to become teachers. Check with an Alexander teacher first to see if your handicap would present a problem in the teaching situation. Of course the Alexander Technique isn't able to stop a degenerative disease like multiple sclerosis, for example, but people with multiple sclerosis have studied and learned how to use their bodies as best they can within their limitations. If you feel motivated to learn how to release excess tension and find out how to be more comfortable in your body, you should not let your handicap stop you from taking lessons.

Do Alexander teachers have to think about their directions, or has it all become automatic for them?

The directions never become fully automatic for anyone. Habits are very ingrained and never completely disappear. However, as a result of intensive training and experience as a teacher, the teacher's body responds very quickly to the directions. Teachers must remind themselves to stay free, especially when they are teaching because whatever is going on in the teacher's body will be communicated through the teacher's hands to the student. Teachers also remind themselves throughout the day, but it does not feel like a chore because when you direct it makes things easier.

When you are not directing but simply carrying out an activity, you are operating with what Alexander called a "standard of use." When you first begin to study the technique, your standard of use is usually not very good, even if your use is good when you direct. By the time you are an experienced teacher, your standard of use is very good, so that even if you are not thinking about Alexander, your body will be free. However, even then, if you choose to think the directions, you can become even more free.

In addition to working on themselves in daily activity, during lessons, and in lying down work, most teachers take lessons with other teachers occasionally or exchange work with other teachers to keep their teaching skills in top form.

What kind of training should my Alexander teacher have had?

The teacher you study with should be certified. A certified teacher is one who has graduated from a teacher training program that has been approved by the North American Society of Teachers of the Alexander Technique (NASTAT), the national organization that sets professional standards. There are similar groups in Great Britain, Canada, Australia, and Switzerland. The Society ensures that each member has graduated from a qualified training program. These programs are 1,600 hours in length and take place over a period of three years. The ratio of teachers to students in a certified training program has to be five to one. Any teacher you work with should have a certificate from a qualified training program; most qualified teachers will also belong to NASTAT.

How do I find a NASTAT certified teacher?

It's usually best to get a referral from someone you know who has worked with a teacher or from a professional such as doctor, physical therapist, chiropractor, or massage therapist. If you don't know anyone who has studied the technique, contact NASTAT for a list of teachers:

North American Society of Teachers of the
Alexander Technique (NASTAT)

P.O. Box 806, Ansonia Station
New York, NY 10023-0806

212-866-5640

If you live in the New York City area, contact the American Center for the Alexander Technique. ACAT is the oldest teacher training program in the United States and was cofounded by Judith. It maintains a list of all of its alumni, all of whom are certified teachers of the technique.

The American Center for the Alexander
  Technique (ACAT)
129 West 67th Street
New York, NY 10023-9998

212-799-0468

How can I study the Alexander Technique if there isn't a certified teacher in my area?

If your area does not have an Alexander teacher, we encourage you to read everything you can about the Alexander Technique. Some individuals have organized groups of people interested in learning the Alexander Technique and brought an Alexander teacher to their community to teach an intensive workshop or give private lessons. If the endeavor is successful, you can have the teacher travel to you on a regular basis. Contact NASTAT to get a list of teachers who travel.

How do you know when you have had enough lessons?

Again, this depends on you. Some people find that thirty lessons are enough for what they want to know. Others study for much longer periods of time. It depends entirely on how much you would like to learn. The Alexander Technique is a process, an upward spiral of learning. In a spiral, the general direction is up, but there will be plateaus or times when you feel that you may be regressing. These times are inevitable. It would be wonderful if each lesson took up precisely where the last left off and the movement was always forward, but it doesn't work that way. However, these down times or plateaus are often the prelude to a new spurt of learning, so try not to get too discouraged.

Your teacher will help guide you in your decision of when to stop. Some people prefer to study for a long time with no breaks; others like to take breaks and then come back. However, you need to have solid base of learning before taking a break; we recommend that you have at least thirty lessons as a solid base.

Why do I feel a little scared about beginning lessons?

In changing the shape of our bodies, we can't help but change our self-image. As you begin to learn the Alexander Technique, you might feel a fear of the unknown: fear that the new body use will be no better than the old, that the technique won't work, fear of giving up parts of yourself—even if they are inefficient movement habits that should be changed. Feelings of insecurity can be alleviated by reminding yourself that you are experimenting—just trying something on for size. You can always return to where you were. If your primary concern is "getting it right," you won't be able to take chances, and taking chances is necessary for change to take place. Trying something different should be fun!

PART II

The Leibowitz Procedures

The Leibowitz Procedures ⟋

The Leibowitz Procedures are a series of movements that Judith developed while working in the Drama Division at The Juilliard School. Until that time, the Alexander Technique had always been taught in one-on-one private lessons. In the Drama Division, Judith had classes that consisted of six to eight students in a group. Since she could work on only one student at a time, she wanted to give the other students something to do while she worked on one person. Based on movement problems students were having in their voice, movement, or dance classes and in everyday life, Judith developed a series of simple movements that students could work on individually as she worked with someone else. These movements are the Leibowitz Procedures. Her repertoire grew steadily into the program that she continues to teach at The Juilliard School today.

The Alexander Technique is taught during the whole four-year program in the Drama Division of The Juilliard School. In the first two years the students meet twice a week in small group classes of six. In addition, once every three weeks each student has a private lesson. In the third and fourth years the students have periodic private lessons and an occasional small group class. The students are expected to apply what they learn in class to their other classes in speech, voice, movement, dance, and acting, as well as to their stage work. By the end of the four years, the drama students have had an intensive course of Alexander lessons.

You must remember that the Leibowitz Procedures and the Alexander Technique are not the same thing. The procedures are a *series of movements* that are designed to help you observe yourself objectively in movement and at rest and to help you learn how the body moves when it is used well. The Alexander Technique is a method for learning how to inhibit old movement patterns and replacing them by consciously directing yourself into new patterns of behavior. The Alexander Technique is not a series of movements or exercises. To learn the Alexander Technique you must have the guidance of a certified Alexander Teacher who can guide you into new experiences in your body. We have included the Leibowitz Procedures in this book because we realize that not everyone has access to an Alexander teacher, and we wanted to give you ways of helping yourself improve your functioning.

The Leibowitz Procedures include some of our most basic movements. You will be shown how to reach, bend, lift, walk, and carry out other activities with the best possible body mechanics and with freedom in the muscles and joints.

Don't try to do the procedures all at once. If you try to learn them too quickly you may use excess effort. We recommend learning one procedure at a time. Take all the time you need to read the instructions. Then try the procedure in front of a mirror. Then go back and read the directions again before trying again. One or two procedures a day is enough.

On the second day, start by reviewing the instructions from the first day and watch yourself carry them out in the mirror before going on to the next procedure.

Pay attention to what Alexander called "the critical moment." He found in working on himself that he was able to inhibit his old habits and think his directions right up to the moment when he actually began to move (the critical moment). But as soon as he began to move he lost his inhibition and direction and fell back into his old habits. After a great deal of experimentation, he found that to carry out the activity successfully he had to focus on the process of the movement and continue to think the directions throughout the movement. As you work through these procedures, remember to take the time to inhibit and direct, then continue to direct through the critical moment and throughout the movement.

Remember that the purpose is to apply the procedures in your daily life. For example, once you learn how to bend easily through your practice in the procedures, begin to bend that way in your everyday life. Although you won't always remember to do it, the more you remind yourself and do it consciously, the faster it will become more natural to you.

OBSERVING YOURSELF IN THE MIRROR ✍

Your first step is to become acquainted with working in front of a full-length mirror, or, if you are lucky enough to have one, a three-way mirror. Stand far enough away from the mirror so that you can see your whole body. We know how difficult it can be to look at yourself, but make the effort to observe yourself closely and objectively. It is important to look at yourself without making critical judgments. Usually our initial response when looking in a mirror is to "fix" something—to adjust the hair, push the shoulders back, or suck the stomach in. Rather than making adjustments, study your mirror image as though it were someone else. You want to see your image as a whole —from head to toe—rather than as disparate parts (e.g., shoulders, head, waist, legs).

The mirror is a tool to help you recognize and work with faulty sensory perception. Wrong can feel right. You may feel quite straight, but when observing yourself in the mirror you may see that one of your shoulders is higher than the other, your lower back is overarched, your neck is jutting forward, and so on. Just as Alexander could clearly see the misuse he could not feel, you may also see in the mirror what you do not feel. As you become more expert at objective self-observation, the mirror will be your guide in helping you recognize whether or not you are carrying out your objectives (e.g., maintaining the poise of your head and the lengthening of your spine in movement). The mirror will help you bring about change more quickly and efficiently.

Think of your muscular system as an envelope in which your skeleton is enclosed. If the envelope is too small for the enclosure, your internal organs will be compressed and your skeleton misshapen. Studying your mirror image, visualize how your muscular system may be distorting your skeleton. You will probably not have sudden insights while studying yourself. You are more likely to gradually recognize your patterns and understand how they must change.

Before you begin the movement procedures, take a few moments to stand in front of the mirror and look at yourself from head to toe. First get a general sense of yourself as a totality; then ask yourself these questions about specific parts.

Head

Where is my head in relation to my neck?

- Is my head pressing back and down?
- Is my head tucked too far down and in?
- Does my jaw jut forward?
- Is my chin compressed into my neck?

How does my head sit on top of my spine?

- Is my head tilted to one side?
- Is my head a little twisted when the rest of my body faces straight toward the mirror?

Upper Torso

Where is my neck in relation to the rest of my spine?

- Is my neck jutting out in front of my body?
- Is my neck pushed too far back so that it is overly straight?
- Is my neck tilted to one side?

What are my shoulders doing?

- Are they hiked up toward my ears?
- Are they rounded forward?
- Are they pinched back?
- Are they level?

What is happening in my chest and rib cage?

- Is my rib cage pulled too far forward?
- Are my ribs sunken?
- Are my the ribs held up rigidly?

Lower Torso

What is happening in my lower back?

- Is it overarched?
- Is it overly flattened?

What is my stomach doing?

- Is it sticking out too far?
- Am I sucking it in too hard?

How about my pelvis?

- Is it tilted forward or back?
- Is it twisted to one side?
- Is one hip higher than the other?

Extremities

What is happening with my arms?

- Are they hanging level?
- Are they twisted too far in or out?
- Are they held crooked at the elbows?

What are my legs doing?

- Are my knees braced back?
- Are my knees unnecessarily bent?
- Are my feet toed in, toed out, or pointing straight forward?

Remember to be objective and nonjudgmental in your observations. Take in what you see without doing anything to change it.

Note: If you are in pain, do only the lying down and breathing procedures. These are very gentle and should help ease your back. When you feel better you can try the other procedures. If you feel uncomfortable while doing any procedure, stop. Always consult with your physician before undertaking any new movement program.

The Leibowitz Procedures are movement procedures; we are not dealing with set positions or postures. When you look at the illustrations, remember that they represent one moment in a continuous movement, not a static position. Within your basic body build, the shape of your body is largely determined by the shape of your movement (how your movement is carried out). For example, you may use your arms in a way that puts pressure down the back, pulls the lower ribs too far forward, and exaggerates your lumbar curve. If you want to change the shape of your body, you must recognize how you move and, using the Alexander principles, while carrying out the procedures, change the movement that is distorting your body. The following procedures are designed to help you learn how to change your movement.

Remember that you are practicing inhibition and direction at all times while you are doing the procedures. Your objective is to maintain the poise of your head and the lengthening of your spine in movement and at rest. Remember not to "position" your head or try to force length and width. Lengthening and widening in the torso come from an internal release, which results from inhibiting the old habit.

Moving Your Hand to Move Your Arm

1. Stand facing the mirror with your feet comfortably apart. Observe yourself in the

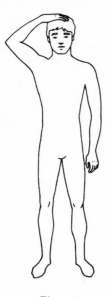

Figure 8

mirror. Your face should be perpendicular to the floor.

2. Inhibit: Say no to compressing your head down on your spine.

3. Continue to say no to pressing your head down on your spine. Think your directions: *Let my neck be free, to let my head go forward and up, to let my torso lengthen and widen, to let my legs release away from my torso, and let my shoulders widen out to the sides.*

4. Continue to think the directions as you begin to move. Let the fingers of your right hand lead your whole arm upward into movement, almost as though you were a marionette and invisible strings were pulling your arm into movement. Rest your palm on top of your head. (See Figure 8.)

5. Rethink the directions.

6. As your head remains poised and your spine remains lengthened, let your fingers lead your arm down so that it rests by your side.

7. Repeat the steps with your other arm.

It's important to observe yourself as you make this movement. Make sure that your head does not pull back and down as you raise your arm. Your head should not pull to one side or the other as your arm goes up. Try this procedure standing in profile and check to make sure that you don't arch your lower back or push your shoulders back when you move your arm. The movement should not be initiated by hiking your shoulder but should begin in the finger-tips. This is an image; there are no muscles in your fingers that can raise your arm—the muscles that raise your arm are actually in your upper arm and shoulder —but we have found that the image of starting the movement at the fingers helps to free the movement from the old habit.

When you are able to raise your arm without compressing your head, using unnecessary tension in your shoulder, or arching your lower back, try raising both arms at once. Be careful! It's quite a challenge to raise both arms without arching your back.

Raising Your Arm, Part 1

1. Face the mirror with your feet comfortably apart.

2. Inhibit and direct: *Let my neck be free, to let my head go forward and up, to let my torso lengthen and widen, to let my legs release away from my torso, and let my shoulders widen.*

3. As you continue to direct, let the fingers of your right hand lead your hand up and place the palm on the back of your neck at the base of your skull. Let your hand be soft so that you can feel any tension in your neck.

4. Let the fingers of your left hand lead your arm straight up toward the ceiling so that your fingers and arm are extended. (See Figure 9.)

5. Continue to think the poise of your head and the length and the width of your torso as you lead with your fingers to bring your left arm down, and then bring your right arm down.

6. Repeat with your left hand at the base of your skull.

Your hand is at the base of your skull to feel if you are pulling your head back and down. Also, make sure that you don't pull your chin toward your neck.

Figure 9

Watch yourself in the mirror throughout the movement to make sure that your spine stays centered. We give you the image of your fingers leading your arm into movement so that you don't initiate movement by lifting your shoulder. The objective is to stay as free as possible in your neck, shoulders, elbows, wrists, and fingers as you move. Your arm should move freely in the shoulder joint—its movement should not disturb the integrity of your torso.

Let's repeat the movement, but this time check yourself at a different point.

Raising Your Arm, Part 2

1. Face the mirror with your feet comfortably apart.

2. Inhibit and direct: *Let my neck be free, to let my head go forward and up, to let my torso lengthen and widen, to let my legs release away from my torso, and let my shoulders widen.* In the mirror, see your spine as the central axis of your torso, with your head poised and centered on your axis.

3. Continue to direct as you let the fingers of your right hand lead your arm behind your back. Place your hand with your palm facing out underneath your left shoulder blade.

4. Direct the fingers of your left hand to raise it sideways toward the ceiling fully extended. (See Figure 10.)

5. Let your left arm come down. Then let your other arm come down.

6. Repeat the movement with your left hand below the right scapula.

Your right hand is placed below your left shoulder blade to make sure that you are not pressing

Figure 10

down when you raise your arm. Your shoulder blade will rise slightly when your arm is fully extended. Your hand is also there to monitor whether your ribs pull forward. Your ribs do not have to change position when your arm is raised. Watch yourself in the mirror to maintain the poise of your head and your central axis as you make the movement.

Raising Both Your Arms

1. Stand facing the mirror with your feet comfortably apart.

2. Inhibit and direct: *Let my neck be free, to let my head go forward and up, to let my torso lengthen and widen, to let my legs release away from my torso, and let my shoulders widen.* Check your central axis and your poised head.

Figure 11

3. Watching to make certain that you maintain your central axis and your poised head, let your fingers lead your arms up until they are fully extended toward the ceiling. (See Figure 11.) Do not pull your ribs forward.

4. Still thinking your head forward and up and seeing that your head remains poised and your axis is centered, lead with your fingers to bring your arms down.

APPLICATION

- Stand facing the mirror. Inhibit and direct. Place a nearly weightless object such as an envelope on the upraised palm of one hand. Leading with your fingers, move your hand to move your arm. What is on your palm will be effortlessly moved with the movement of your hand and arm.
- Stand facing the mirror. Place a light

object on a table or stool nearby (so that you don't have to bend to pick it up). Use an average size book or other unbreakable object. Inhibit and direct. Look at yourself and the object reflected in the mirror. Watch your fingers lead your arm toward the object in the mirror. Let your fingers and thumb make contact with the object. Continuing to watch in the mirror and thinking the directions, move your hand to move your arm to lift the object. Then put it down. As you practice this movement, experiment to see how little muscular support (tension) is needed to move a light object.

Repeat this procedure with heavier objects. Notice whether you anticipate the weight of the object with a compression of your head down on your torso and a tightening of your body. If you are using only one hand to pick up an object, your other hand can go to the back of your neck at the base of your skull to check yourself.

Inhibit any desire to prepare to do the movement. Preparation usually entails a subtle form of tensing. Instead, think the Alexander directions. Be willing not to pick up the object. It may not feel possible to pick it up without your habitual tensions. Continuing to think the directions, bring your hand to the object, allowing your body intelligence to determine what the necessary support should be. *Tension has weight*. If you introduce undue tension, you are adding the weight of your tensions to the weight of the object.

We are constantly lifting and moving various objects in space. We lift food to our mouths and combs to our hair. We lift books, newspapers, television remotes, keys, pens and pencils, glasses, makeup, toothbrushes, and so on. This offers us many opportunities to examine how we carry out these activities and to change what we choose.

- Stand facing the mirror holding a comb or brush. Inhibit and direct. Maintaining your spinal lengthening and the poise of your head, let your fingers lead your arm up to your hair. Comb your hair as you continue to let your neck be free, to let your head go forward and up, to let your torso lengthen and widen. Leave your shoulders free. Make sure that your neck doesn't tighten unnecessarily. Try it again with a toothbrush, with makeup, or a razor. These are all good activities to try since you usually do them in front of a mirror.

Head Movements

1. Stand facing the mirror with your feet comfortably apart. Observe yourself in the mirror. Visualize a central axis running through your body, with your head centered and poised on the axis.

2. Inhibit: Say no to your head pressing down on your spine.

3. Think your directions: *Let my neck be free, to let my head go forward and up, to let my torso lengthen and widen, to let my legs release away from my torso, and let my shoulders widen.*

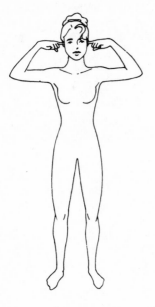

Figure 12

4. Continue to inhibit and direct as you bring a finger up to each ear (see Raising Your Arm on pages 111–13). (See Figure 12.)

5. Imagine your fingers growing through your head and meeting to form a rod, like the rod of a hinge. Everything above the rod is your head; everything below the rod is your neck; and everything in front of the rod is your jaw. No matter what movement you make with your head, this imaginary rod will prevent your head from pressing down and compressing your spine.

6. Thinking your directions, bring your arms down.

Horizontal Head Movement

1. Inhibit and think the directions: *Let my neck be free, to let my head go forward and up, to let my torso lengthen and widen, to let my legs release away from my torso, and let my shoulders widen.*

2. Turn your head to the right, making sure that your nose moves in a line parallel to the floor. This insures that your head doesn't tilt to one side.

3. Bring your head back to center.

4. Repeat as you move your head to the left.

Vertical Head Movement

LOOKING UP

1. Inhibit and think the directions: *Let my neck be free, to let my head go forward and up, to*

let my torso lengthen and widen, to let my legs release away from my torso, and let my shoulders widen. Imagine the rod running through your ears. The imaginary rod will help you move your head without compressing your neck.

2. Leading with a finger, gently bring your finger to the little hollow at the base of your skull. Raise your eyes toward the ceiling, and let your head follow in the upward direction so that your head is tilting up toward the ceiling. Your head rotates on the imaginary rod running through your ears. (See Figure 13.) The movement of your head doesn't compress your spine.

3. Rethink the directions. Continue to think of your head rotating on the rod. Let your eyes lead your head down so that you are facing straight forward. You should feel no pressure on your finger at the base of your skull.

4. Bring your finger down.

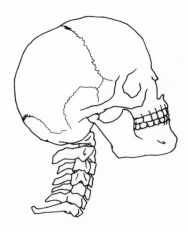

Figure 13

LOOKING DOWN

1. Inhibit and think the directions: *Let my neck be free, to let my head go forward and up, to let my torso lengthen and widen, to let my legs release away from my torso, and let my shoulders widen.* Imagine the rod running through your ears.

2. Leading with a finger, gently bring it to the little hollow at the base of your skull. Let your eyes drop toward the ground and let your head follow down. Your head rotates on the rod as it tilts down. (See Figure 14.)

3. Rethink the directions. Continue to think

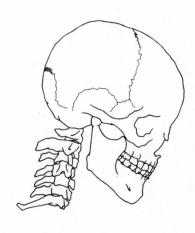

Figure 14

of your head rotating on the rod. Let your eyes lead your head up so that you are facing forward.

4. Bring your finger down.

It is important to remember your directions when moving your head up and down so that you maintain the lengthening and widening torso by preventing your head from pressing down on your neck. You don't want your torso to sink down just because you are moving your head down. When you move your head to look up, make sure that you don't over-arch your lower back. Your head should be able to move independently of your torso.

APPLICATION

- Stand in profile to the mirror. Inhibit and direct. Going through the steps listed above, turn your head to look at your profile in the mirror. Make sure that your neck remains free as you turn. Look straight ahead again.
- Inhibit and direct. Think through the steps listed above in order to look down at your shoes. Redirect to bring your head back to center. Redirect to look up at the ceiling. Redirect to bring your head to center again.
- Inhibit and direct as you walk around the room as though you were walking down a street. Look from side to side and up and down as though you were looking in shop windows, looking at the ground, looking up at buildings, and checking traffic lights. Really look around and see the room. Continue to direct as you walk and move your head.

- (This application uses the head and arm procedures.) Let your fingers lead your arm to the telephone and take hold of the receiver between your fingers and thumb. The receiver now becomes an extension of your hand, as you move your hand, the phone will come with it. Instead of bringing your head down to the phone, bring the phone up to your head. Maintain your upward direction as you speak on the phone and as your hand leads the receiver down.

Vertical Bending, Part 1

1. Stand facing the mirror with your feet comfortably apart and slightly turned out.

2. Inhibit and direct: *Let my neck be free, to let my head go forward and up, to let my torso lengthen and widen, to let my legs release away from my torso, and let my shoulders widen.* See your head poised on your spine in the mirror. Ask your torso to release into length and width in the direction of your head. You are opening into your full dimensions—making room for your bones.

3. Look at the mirror and locate the central axis of your body (your spine). It runs up from the bottom of your torso to your head. Your head is centered on the axis. See your face perpendicular to the floor.

4. Continue to think these thoughts as you watch your central axis lower approximately six inches as you bend your knees over your toes. Direct the poise of your head and the length through your spine as you bend your knees. (See Figure 15.)

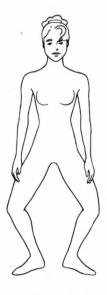

Figure 15

5. Rethink the directions.

6. Maintaining the length of your torso, see your head lead your central axis up as you straighten your knees.

No matter what direction your body moves in space, the energy flow in your torso should be toward your head. By tensing the muscles of your body, you make your body heavier, and that weight pulls you down. If you release the excess tension, you will literally become lighter; you'll have more room for your internal organs, and your blood will circulate more easily. An "energy flow up" also means a willingness to let your body take up its full space—to move up out of yourself rather than pull down into yourself—so you have more direct contact with the world around you. In other words, an energy flow is also an attitude.

As you bend vertically, your torso should maintain its length. You move downward in space because you shorten the distance between your hip joint and the floor by bending your knees over your toes. Movement takes place at the hip, knee, and ankle joints. There should be no change in the poise of your head or in your lower back.

Vertical Bending, Part 2

1. Stand facing the mirror with your feet comfortably apart and slightly turned out.

2. Inhibit and direct: *Let my neck be free, to let my head go forward and up to let my torso lengthen and widen, to let my legs release away from my torso, and let my shoulders widen.* Find your central axis in the mirror.

3. Continue inhibiting and directing as you bring one hand to your lower back, palm facing outward (see procedures for use of

hands and arms), and the other hand (palm facing inward) to your hip joint in front. (See Figure 16.) Your hands are there to make sure that you don't overarch your middle back or tuck your pelvis under.

4. Maintaining the poise of your head and the lengthening of your spine, continue to think the directions as you watch your central axis lower by bending your knees over your toes. There should be no change in your middle back between your hands.

Gradually you can increase the depth of the bend.

Figure 16

Bending Your Knees and Inclining Forward

1. Stand with your feet comfortably apart and slightly turned out.

2. Inhibit and direct: *Let my neck be free, to let my head go forward and up, to let my torso lengthen and widen, to let my legs release away from my torso, and let my shoulders widen.* Find your central axis in the mirror and see your head poised at the top of your spine.

3. Lead with your hand to bring your hands to the greater trochanter. (See Figure 17.) Imagine your fingers growing across your torso to meet and form a rod, like the rod of a hinge. The rod runs through your hip joint. Everything above this imaginary rod is your torso, and everything below is your leg.

4. Continue to direct and bend your knees.

5. Let your torso incline forward from your hip joints by thinking of rotating your torso on the imaginary rod. You bend where your hands are placed. (See Figure 18.)

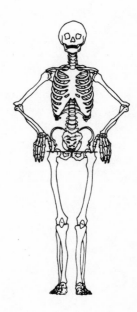

Figure 17

Figure 18

6. Think of your head as leading your lengthening spine as you rotate your torso on the rod. Straighten your knees, and let your arms hang at your sides as you come to your full height.

Whenever you make a bending motion at the hip joints, your torso should release into length toward your head; your legs should release into length toward your knee. We have broken the bending motion into two parts—bending your knees alone and bending your knees and inclining your torso forward—so that you could become more aware of your habits of bending and of any changes that take place. When bending in life, these two parts of the movement happen simultaneously. As you get more used to bending in this fashion, you will find that you can bend your knees and lean forward from your hip sockets at the same time.

When you pivot your torso into a forward bend, you will no longer be able to see the movement in the mirror—your eyes will be looking toward the floor. When you stand up you will be able to look toward the mirror again. Place your hands right above the hip joint to locate where the movement should occur. You can also try the movement with one hand in front on your hip joint and one behind at your lower back to see if you are overarching or overflattening your back.

If you keep your hands soft when placing them at your hip joint and lower back, you are more likely to feel when the lower back overworks. Make sure that your head doesn't pull back and down as you lean forward. Keep your head, neck, and torso in the same relationship when you bend as when you stand. This way of bending is safe and healthy for your back.

Many people bend over from the waist (where

there is no hinge joint), which can harm the lower back. The tiny joints between the vertebrae of your spine, called facet joints, are distortion joints and allow for the movements of twisting and turning. They are not major weight-bearing joints—those are in your legs (your ankle, knee, and hip joints). When bending you should use those three sets of joints. This way of moving may feel unfamiliar at first but will come to feel more natural as you do it.

APPLICATION

- Getting in and out of a chair. We all have particularly strong habits associated with getting in and out of a chair. Knowing that the chair will catch us, we often let ourselves drop into it. Rather than falling into the chair and using excess pressure in your back when standing, think of getting in and out of the chair as another form of bending.

  Place a chair or stool behind you. Stand in front of the mirror and observe the poise of your head on your central axis. Inhibit and direct. As you think of lengthening up, let your knees bend forward over your toes, let your torso incline forward from your hip joint, and continue to let your knees bend until you reach the chair. (See Figure 19.) After you reach the chair, let your torso rotate at your hip sockets so that you are sitting upright in the chair. Next, as you continue to direct yourself up, let your head lead your torso forward from the hip joints. As you pivot forward from your joints, your

Figure 19

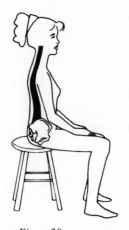

Figure 20

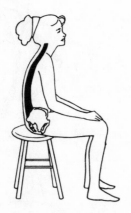

Figure 21

weight will be transferred onto your feet. Press your feet gently into the floor in order to straighten your legs.

Many people overuse their back muscles in getting up from a chair. If your head remains poised and your torso remains lengthened and widened, your back does very little work—your legs will bring you up. Try this procedure in profile so you can check to see that you aren't overarching your back or slumping forward when standing.

Sitting is one of the most difficult tasks you have to perform. There is more pressure on your body when you sit than when you stand. Sitting is an *activity*. To sit well you need to be well balanced on your sitting bones so that the weight of your body is supported by the chair, couch, or stool. Your legs don't have to work when you're sitting, so they should be very free. When you inhibit and direct, the muscles of your torso work together to gently support you. (See Figure 20.) If you let go of your muscles totally, you will slump. (See Figure 21.) When you become adept at inhibition and direction, this gentle work does not feel like a strain; instead, it comes to feel natural and slumping will feel unnatural.

If you need to sit for any length of time, it is best to use a chair with good back support.

• To lean over a sink, go through the steps listed above in order to bend. Maintain the poise of your head and the lengthening and widening of your torso as you lean over the sink. Leading with your hand, bring your hand to the faucet. Take hold of the tap and rotate your wrist to turn it on and wash your hands. Use the same procedure to turn the tap off. Directing yourself, straighten your legs to come up. Lead with your hand to pick up a towel to dry your hands.

Through all of these procedures, the constant is the poise of your head and the lengthening and widening of your torso. This is a thought rather than an action.

Figure 22

Moving Forward and Back in a Chair

1. Sit near the edge of the chair facing the mirror with both feet flat on the floor. Your face is parallel to the mirror (perpendicular to the floor).

2. Inhibit and direct: *Let my neck be free, to let my head go forward and up, to let my torso lengthen and widen, to let my legs release away from my torso, and let my shoulders widen.* Check the poise of your head and the lengthening of your spine in the mirror.

3. As you think the directions and keep your feet firmly planted on the floor, let your torso move back from your hip sockets so that your back is resting on the back of the chair. (See Figure 22.) Your face remains parallel to the mirror.

4. Rethink the directions. Keeping your feet firmly planted and your face parallel to the mirror, allow your head to lead your torso up—rotate on your hip joints so that you are seated vertically again. The abdominal muscles do the work.

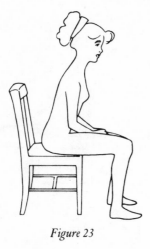

Figure 23

5. Let your head lead your torso into a forward bend (as though you were leaning toward a desk). Let the movement happen at your hip joints. (See Figure 23.)

6. Think the directions as you let your head lead your torso so you are seated vertically again.

Throughout the course of this movement your head remains poised at the top of your spine; your torso is lengthened and widened and moves as a unit from the hip sockets. Your face remains parallel to the mirror as you go from vertical to the back of the chair and back to vertical again. There should be no change in your lumbar spine during the movement.

You can repeat this movement with one hand at your hip socket and the other at your lower back to make sure that you are not overusing your lower back muscles. You can also repeat the movement with one hand at the base of your skull to check the poise of your head, the other hand at your lower back to make sure that you don't pull your head back or overuse your lower back muscles.

We spend a good part of our lives in chairs—at desks, at tables, in armchairs, and in cars. This rocking on your hip joints is a movement you do innumerable times a day. Begin to move at your hip sockets when sitting rather than bending forward from the waist. By moving in this more efficient way, not only will you move with greater freedom, ease, and grace, but you will eliminate the trauma that bending at the waist can cause.

APPLICATION

- Sit at a desk or a table. Inhibit and direct. Going through the steps listed above, move

back and forth from your hip joints to
bring yourself toward and away from the
desk.

- When inclining forward from your hip
  sockets to pick things up on the desk and
  move them, try leading with your hand.
  Maintain the poise of your head and the
  length through your torso as you move
  pencils and paperclips. (See Figure 24.)
- Many chairs and automobile seats incline
  backward. Instead of collapsing through
  your middle to lean back, allow the
  movement to happen at your hip joints as
  you lengthen and widen.

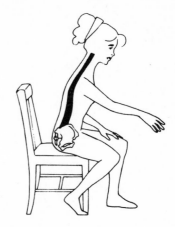

Figure 24

Bending from a Wide Stance, Part 1

For those of you who have taken dance, this is a form
of the second position, plié.

   1. Face the mirror and take a wide stance
with your feet slightly turned out.
   2. Inhibit and direct. *Let my neck be free, to
let my head go forward and up, to let my torso
lengthen and widen, to let my legs release away
from my torso, and let my shoulders widen.* Find
your vertical axis in the mirror.
   3. Allow the vertical axis to come down by
bending your knees over your toes. (See
Figure 25.)
   4. Redirect and press your feet down gently
to straighten your legs. Make sure you don't
arch your back.

Bending from a Wide Stance, Part 2

   1. Inhibit and direct. *Let my neck be free, to
let my head go forward and up, to let my torso*

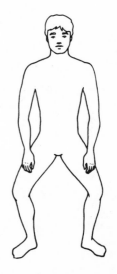

Figure 25

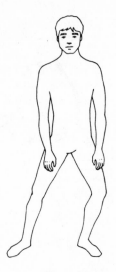

Figure 26

lengthen and widen, to let my legs release away from my torso, and let my shoulders widen. Find your central axis in the mirror.

2. Watch the mirror image move your central axis to the left as you bend your left knee over your left foot. Your right leg remains straight. (See Figure 26.)

3. Bring the axis to the center by gently pressing your left foot down to straighten your leg.

4. Allow your central axis to move to the right by bending your right knee over your right foot. Your left leg remains straight.

5. Bring your axis to the center by gently pressing your right foot down to straighten your leg. It is very important to make sure that your lower back doesn't tighten or overarch as you do this movement.

Lunging

1. Stand in front of the mirror with your feet comfortably apart.

2. Inhibit and direct: *Let my neck be free, to let my head go forward and up, to let my torso lengthen and widen, to let my legs release away from my torso, and let my shoulders widen.* Remember the imaginary rod running through your ears that marks the separation between your head and your neck. Remember the imaginary rod running through your hip sockets that marks the separation between your torso and your legs.

3. As you continue to direct, let your central axis move to the right so that your weight is on your right foot. As you shift your weight, check the mirror to make sure that

your shoulders and pelvis stay level. Don't lift your hip up or bend at the waist when shifting your weight.

4. Let your left knee bend and take a step to the side so that you have a wide stance with your feet turned slightly out.

5. Let your body turn at the ankle joints so that it faces in the direction of your left foot.

6. Thinking of lengthening and widening, let your left knee bend forward and pivot the torso over the imaginary rod. Let your arms hang. Don't bend your right knee and leave the right foot flat on the floor. (See Figure 27.)

7. Straighten your knee as you bring your body upright and face the mirror.

8. Repeat these steps bending your right knee.

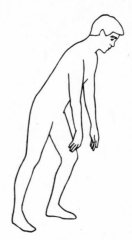

Figure 27

When turning to the right and to the left, free your ankles, knees, and hips to allow the movement to happen on the joints. Incline forward as your knee bends. The lunge is the same bending motion as the bend discussed earlier except that only one of your knees is bent. Check yourself in profile to make sure you are not bending at the waist when making this motion.

This procedure can also be done with one foot placed diagonally in front of the other. (See Figure 28.)

APPLICATION

•   Place two chairs in front of the mirror. Put the chairs four to six feet apart, depending on your height. (The taller you are, the farther apart they should be.) Place an object on the chair to your left. You will be moving the object from that chair to the

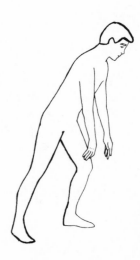

Figure 28

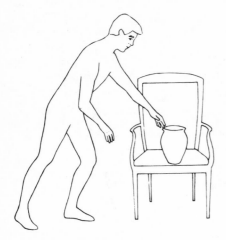

Figure 29

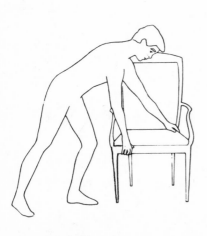

Figure 30

other chair. Stand between the chairs facing the mirror and take a wide stance with your feet comfortably turned out. Inhibit and direct. Look at the object. Let your eyes lead your head into movement. Swivel on your ankles to face the chair, leaving your feet where they were. Redirect. As your hand leads toward the object, let your left knee bend and your torso pivot forward from your hip joints. (See Figure 29.) Take hold of the object. Without increasing the tension in your arm or shoulder ("bracing" to support the object), return to vertical by straightening your knee and unpivoting. Face the mirror. Redirect. Look toward the right chair. Let your body swivel toward the right from the ankle joints. Let your right knee bend and your torso pivot forward as your hand leads toward the chair to put the object down. Redirect as you straighten your knee and unpivot. Face the mirror. (Do not do this if you have back pain. Wait until you feel stronger before you try it.)

- Place one lightweight chair in front of the mirror to your left. Face the mirror. Take a wide stance with your feet comfortably turned out. Inhibit and direct. Let your eyes lead your head to look at the chair. Swivel toward the chair from your ankle joints. Redirect. Let both hands lead toward the chair. At the same time, bend your left knee and let your torso come forward from the hip sockets. Place your hands underneath the chair seat. (See Figure 30.) Inhibit any "preparing" (tensing), and come out of the diagonal bend and let the chair come with you. Straighten your leg and face the mirror. Redirect. Swivel in the opposite direction. Bend your right knee, make a diagonal bend, and place the chair down. Straighten your right knee and face the mirror.

In the lunge you are moving at all the joints of your legs—ankles, knees, and hips. Your elbows should be slightly bent when moving the chair to prevent strain in your shoulders. There should be no compression in the small of your back, at the back of your neck, or across your shoulders. When you are able to do the movement with facility, try picking up the chair and carrying it a few steps before you put it down.

Squatting

This can be a more advanced movement. Do not do it if you are in pain, or have restricted motion.

1. Stand in front of the mirror with your feet wide apart and comfortably turned out. (If you need extra support place a chair in front of you and rest your hands on the back of the chair.)

2. Inhibit and direct: *Let my neck be free, to let my head go forward and up, to let my torso lengthen and widen, to let my legs release away from my torso, and let my shoulders widen.*

3. As you continue to think up, let your knees bend as you incline forward from your hip sockets. Come all the way down into a squat. Leave your hands on the back of the chair and leave your heels down if you can. (See Figure 31.)

Figure 31

4. Redirect.

5. Continue to think your directions as you lean slightly forward and press your feet down gently in order to straighten your legs. Try not to use your hands to pull yourself up.

The squat is a continuation of the bending that we discussed earlier. You go through the same steps that you did for bending. As with the other types of bending, the most important thing is to maintain your upward direction as you go down through space. You go down in space because you are shortening the distance between your hip joint and the floor by bending your knees. The objective is to maintain the poise of your head and the lengthening of your spine in the movement.

Use your hands on the back of the chair to steady yourself if necessary. When you become more proficient, try the movement without the chair.

APPLICATION

Do not do this if you can't squat without support.

- Stand in front of the mirror with your feet comfortably apart and turned out slightly. Place a book on the floor directly in front of you. Inhibit and direct. Go through the steps listed above in order to let your hands lead your arms to pick up the book. Return to standing. Then try it with two, three, and four books—but make sure to maintain good use as you squat.

Walking

1. Stand in front of the mirror.
2. Inhibit and direct: *Let my neck be free, to*

let my head go forward and up, to let my torso lengthen and widen, to let my legs release away from my torso, and let my shoulders widen. Check your central axis in the mirror.

3. Maintain your central vertical axis as movement begins at the back of your left knee. Gently press your toes down to bring your knee forward.

4. Allow your left lower leg to gently swing forward from the knee and land on your heel. Then allow your whole foot to come onto the floor as you take your vertical axis forward; this will trigger your right leg to bend your right knee. Gently push off with your toes and let your right lower leg swing forward to take another step landing on your heel. If you continue to take your central vertical axis forward you will be walking. (See Figure 32.) Make sure not to hike your hip up when bringing your leg forward.

Figure 32

In walking you want to maintain the integrity of your torso and the poise of your head. The movement of your legs carries your torso along. Your torso remains centered and in the line of gravity; it doesn't come too far forward or behind the line of gravity. If your arms hang freely from your shoulder joints, they will swing gently and alternately with each leg. Your knee should bend over your first and second toes.

Lying Down

1. Lie down on a carpeted floor or a mat.
2. Place enough books under your head to ensure that your head is not pressing back and down.
3. Inhibit and direct: *Let my neck be free, to*

let my head go forward and up, to let my torso
lengthen and widen, to let my legs release away
from my torso, and let my shoulders widen.

4. Bend one leg, then the other, so that
your knees are bent toward the ceiling with
your feet flat on the floor. Your feet should be
slightly outside the line of your pelvis. (See
Figure 33.)

5. Place your hands on your rib cage.

6. Continue to think your directions as you
lie there for ten to fifteen minutes.

Figure 33

This procedure is especially helpful when you
are feeling tired, worn out, or tense. When lying
down, you don't have to deal with gravity. Your back
can release and spread out against the floor. However,
make sure that you don't force your back down. Lying
down in this fashion is especially helpful for working
on inhibition. You can really inhibit your movement
habits when you aren't moving!

Do remind yourself about the directions when
you are lying down. You will be less apt to "try and
make them happen" when lying down. Even if it
doesn't feel as if anything is happening, something *is*
happening if you are directing. You are educating your
nervous system and muscles by telling them to do
something different—to release. Releasing is not the
same as relaxing. Releasing means letting go of excess
tension so that you are energized for activity; relaxing
means completely letting go and ending up like a rag
doll. We are interested in getting you released so that

you will feel refreshed, even after just ten to fifteen minutes of this kind of lying down work.

While lying down you may want to think "to let my head go forward and out" rather than "forward and up." Since you are lying down, you want your head and spine to release in the direction parallel to the floor rather than up toward the ceiling. The head leads the spine into length, whatever position you are in. If you are vertical, you will release straight up toward the ceiling; if you are in a bend, for example, the "up" direction is a diagonal.

Breathing

1. Lie down and bring your knees up as described above. Place your hands on your rib cage.

2. Inhibit and direct: *Let my neck be free, to let my head go forward and up, to let my torso lengthen and widen, to let my legs release away from my torso, and let my shoulders widen.*

3. Notice your breathing *without changing it.*

4. If your breathing seems shallow or difficult, inhibit holding your breath.

5. Continue to direct, adding the direction to release the muscles between your ribs (on the front, back, and sides of your body).

Make sure when you think about breathing that you don't "do" anything. You are undoing, rather than doing. If your breathing is difficult, tense, or shallow, you have tension in your body. Inhibiting and directing will improve your breathing, but directing your attention to your breathing will improve it even more. It is important first to simply observe your breathing and inhibit the desire to change it—to take larger breaths, to suck in air, to force your ribs out, and so on. Just notice. Then ask yourself not to hold your breath. People often unconsciously hold their breath when performing simple activities, especially in difficult and stressful circumstances. As your middle and lower back release toward the floor, your lower ribs will also drop. This allows your diaphragm and your intercostal muscles to do their job more efficiently. Make sure you don't force your back toward the floor. Think of your breath dropping into your lower back.

APPLICATION

- When you are lying in bed before you go to sleep, say your directions. Notice your breathing and ask yourself not to hold your breath. Let the tensions of the day leave your body.

Speaking

This procedure can be done either standing or sitting facing the mirror.

1. See your central axis with your head poised on top. Inhibit and direct: *Let my neck be free, to let my head go forward and up, to let my torso lengthen and widen, to let my legs release away from my torso, and let my shoulders widen.*
2. Continue to think the directions. Lead with your hand and place it at the base of your skull. Check to see that there is no change in the poise of your head as you do the procedure.
3. Notice your breathing. There should be no compression at the base of your skull during inhalation and exhalation. Check to see that your face remains perpendicular to the

floor and your eye level remains the same as you open and close your mouth.

4. Continue to direct as you open your mouth and let the air out on the extended vowel sound *ah*. Make sure that you don't compress as you do this.

5. Close your mouth, and allow the air to enter your nose without sniffing. It should happen lightly and easily. Open your mouth and let out another vowel sound. Repeat. Try other extended vowel sounds. Eventually you can begin to say words. Make sure that your neck doesn't tighten as you talk.

When doing this procedure, don't suck air in or use more air than you need—the air should flow in very gently. Direct your lips, mouth, and tongue to be free as you open and close your mouth. It helps to think of an open hollow tube that goes from your mouth down to your lungs and allows for a free flow of air.

Your larynx or voice box is in your throat, so any tightening in the throat will change the sound of your voice. Voices can sound overly breathy, strained, muffled, tense, or controlled if the throat is tight. The other major factor that affects the way the voice sounds is your breathing. Many of us breathe shallowly and often hold our breath unconsciously in certain situations. The solution is *not* to take a deep breath. When you take a deep breath, almost invariably you suck in air through your nose (which actually closes and tightens the nasal passages) and lift your chest, forcing air into your lungs. Taking air into your lungs in such a forceful way is not desirable.

Become aware of how you are breathing in daily life. Check during the day to determine if you are holding your breath. If you find that you are, ask yourself to stop, and your breathing will kick in automatically. Thinking the directions will help keep your throat and rib cage free. Also become aware of your voice as you go about your daily activities. Listen to the sound of it. If you catch yourself straining, think your directions. If you can't hear how your body affects the sound of your voice, pull your head back and down and slump, read aloud, and listen to yourself. Then release up into your full length and continue reading. Your voice should sound freer and clearer than when you were slumping.

APPLICATION

- Begin to notice how you use your voice in everyday life. Does it seem to be habitually loud, soft, breathy, or harsh? Do you tend to hold your breath or to breathe in a shallow manner, especially in difficult situations? Do you tend to tense your jaw or tongue? These things will restrict your voice. As you work with inhibition and direction and this new awareness of how you are using your voice, you will begin to free it.

Applying the Leibowitz Procedures to Daily Activities ◡

When you feel familiar with the Leibowitz Procedures you can begin to apply the movements to your activities throughout the day. The procedures cover most of the basic movements we have to make in life: reaching, bending, squatting, and lunging. In this chapter we cover some of the activities that you do at home and at work, but you can apply the procedures to any situation. Perhaps the most important element in changing how you do things is self-observation. Rather than mechanically going through the movements we suggest, try to slow down and take time to see what you are doing with yourself. Check yourself in the mirror to see if what you think you are doing is what you are actually doing. If you see something that you think looks tight, make sure that you go back to inhibition and direction rather than just adjusting your body parts. Remember that it's possible to have good alignment and still be using excess tension to maintain that posture. You want to make whatever movements are necessary to carry out an activity with the least possible amount of body effort. When you are unsure about how to make one of the movements, refer back to the preceding chapter.

Some of the main postural habits to look out for when you are carrying out your activities are:

- Head pulling back and down
- Neck pulling too far forward
- Shoulders hunching up, rounding forward, or pushed too far back
- Bending forward from the waist
- Overarching at the lower back
- Overstiffening of the hands and arms
- Locking at the knees

Listed below are several activities to which you can apply the Leibowitz Procedures.

SITTING AT A DESK OR TABLE ∽

Sitting is one of the most difficult things that we must do; it is harder on the body than standing. Many people spend most of their working lives sitting, yet they have never stopped to consider whether the chairs they sit in are appropriate for their bodies, whether their working areas are organized so that they can reach things easily, and most importantly, what they are doing with themselves as they sit.

When you sit, make sure that you let the chair support you. Most often people will do one of two things: either slouch or not allow their body weight to be taken by the chair or hold themselves up too much. If you are going to be working for any length of time, especially if you are at a desk all day, you need back support. Let your body weight go down through your sitting bones and the weight of your back be taken by the back of the chair. To do this, your chair should be quite close to the desk so you can maintain your spinal lengthening. Alternatively, you can lean forward from your hip joints to work at your desk. This can feel very beneficial since it gives a slight stretch to the lower back, but it is difficult to maintain for long periods. You may switch back and forth between the two ways of sitting to keep yourself from becoming too static. Also, check that the height of the table or desk is a good one for you. What's the right height? You should be able to sit at your desk comfortably—it should be neither too high nor too low. If it is too low, you will stoop over the desk. If the desk is too high, you will be unable to rest your arms on the desk, which may lead to tired arms. In addition, your chair should be able to fit underneath the desk. You must be able to pull your chair close to the desk so that you can work there easily, without hunching over. When you sit in the chair your feet should be flat on the floor. The back of the chair should give you proper back support. Do not use a chair with an adjustable back if it moves when you lean against it. The depth of the chair should be correct for you so that you can sit in it without slumping. If it is too deep, use a pillow to support your back—sitting at a desk with nothing to support you is too tiring. You may choose to use a lumbar pillow support when working at your desk. Finally, the chair should have arms so you may rest your arms when working.

If your chair at work is bad, you must get a new one. We realize this is sometimes a problem, but you spend many hours of your day sitting at the office and you need to maintain good body use while you are there. After all, if you are more comfortable, you will work better. If you absolutely cannot get a proper chair from your organization, bring one in yourself. It need not be an expensive one—a plain straight-back chair with a seat that is parallel to the floor (not tilted back) is all you need. You can strap on a lumbar back support and a firm pillow for the seat to make it more comfortable.

People often ask us about the new "kneeling chairs." They have no backs to slump against and so encourage spinal lengthening. Some people find these chairs comfortable and others do not. If you have problems with your knees or shins, do not use one; the slight pressure on the lower part of your leg will be uncomfortable for you. Those chairs are also a little awkward if you have to get up quickly. Some of the chairs are much better made than others. If you are considering buying one, be sure that you sit in one for a long time in the store before making the investment.

There may be times when you are away from your home or office and have to work with furniture that is less than ideal. Try not to give in to poor body use; do what you can to make the furniture work for you. If the chair is too tall for you, place a footstool or books under your feet. Place pillows or your sweater, coat, or purse behind your back for support if necessary.

If you are studying and find that you keep slumping down toward your books, prop them up so that you can read without compressing toward the book. If you spend a lot of time reading books at a desk, you may want to buy a special book stand for this purpose.

Make sure that you take frequent breaks when working. Get up out of your chair and walk around— go to the bathroom or the water cooler. Ideally you should not sit longer than half an hour at a time. Some people feel that they don't want to break their concentration: We caution you that if you don't break your concentration, your body may force you to.

More and more people have to sit and use computers at work or at home. If you use a computer, you must make sure that your desk height is right for you so that your arms are at a comfortable level. If the computer or keyboard seems too low, you can make it higher by simply putting it on a box or pile of books. If it seems too high, find another surface to put it on. Ideally your chair should have arms so that you can rest your arms while you type; holding your arms up for hours can be draining. We want to emphasize again that the chair should give proper back support and proper support at the seat. Use a chair with an adjustable back only if you can make it rigid. If you don't already have one, get a stand that holds paper at eye level next to the machine so you don't have to crane your neck down to see what you are typing. Adequate light is important for the same reason; if there isn't enough, you will probably hunch your body forward to see what you are doing. When typing, maintain your directions while you keep your shoulders, arms, and hands free. In addition, see how little effort you can expend when you hit the keys, as this will help save your energy.

WRITING ✑

Changing your habits of writing is challenging because it is so closely allied with who you are. Learning to write is stressful for most young children, so it is often done with excess tension. The body remembers this tension and is never taught to write another way; consequently most people write with tight hands, wrists, arms, and backs. The whole body can curl up into a tight knot just to write a letter. When writing, focus on your head, neck, and torso integration, and leave your fingers, wrist, and arm free. See how lightly you can hold the pen. Your writing will change and may look messier and less controlled to you, but it probably doesn't look as bad as you think. This should help reduce or eliminate writer's cramp, and the less force you give out, the more energy you will save. If you write or read sitting in an armchair, put a pillow under the book or pad to bring it closer to you.

TALKING ON THE TELEPHONE ✍

If you spend a good deal of time on the telephone, we recommend that you get a headset similar to the kind telephone operators use, since they are lightweight and leave your hands free. Some people may feel that they look funny wearing them, but many executives and Wall Street brokers who spend a lot of time on the phone are now using them. Even if you don't spend all day on the telephone you should consider buying one. We all end up in the strangest positions when on the telephone—craning and straining the neck and shoulders. Also, it is quite difficult to hold up your arm for a long time without pulling your body down toward the phone. When you are holding a regular phone receiver, remember your spinal lengthening as you talk.

FILING ✍

Filing cabinets can be anywhere: high, low, and in between. When bending down to a low filing cabinet, remember to follow the procedures laid out in the last chapter. Bend from the knees and hips rather than hunching over from the waist. If the drawer is very low, it is best for your back if you squat all the way down. This may not sound comfortable for women in tight skirts and high heels, but it will work as long you remember to lengthen as you go down. If you keep your feet close together, you won't have a problem

Figure 34

going down. To get closer to the drawer, you may wish to go down to the drawer in a slight twist. (See Figure 34.) If you need to reach up to a file drawer above you, make sure that you don't arch at your lower back.

ARRANGING YOUR WORK SPACE ❧

There is a new group of professionals called ergonomic engineers. Ergonomics is the study of the spatial relationships between humans and equipment. American businesses have realized that, especially with the advent of the computer age, good ergonomics are essential. Billions of dollars are lost every year through the second leading cause of lost work time: back pain. Anything that businesses can do to reduce this sick time is worth their while, so ergonomic engineers are hired to design work spaces for optimum efficiency and "user friendliness." We want you to take the time to be your own ergonomic consultant.

Set aside a few hours one day to arrange your work space. Make a list of the tasks you perform in the space; then put them in order of priority. Make sure that all the equipment, books, files, notes, and materials you need are easy to reach. The materials that you don't use as often can be put away. Decide if you need anything to help make your physical life simpler and easier: a new chair, a table that is the right height, a step stool or small ladder to get to high files or shelves, additional lighting, a footstool for a chair that's too high, a typing table on wheels so you don't have to lug the typewriter around, storage baskets on wheels, and so on. Try to eliminate work situations where you must stoop, slump, or reach awkwardly across things throughout the day. Use your imagination to arrange things so that your important tools are right at your fingertips and everything else can be found with a minimum of reaching and bending.

DRIVING ✑

Figure 35

It is important to have support for your lower back in your car. We recommend that you get a back support. This is especially important in cars that have seats that lean back; these seats will lead you to slump unless you have help to keep you vertical. There should be enough head room so you don't have to slouch, and the seat should be pulled forward far enough so that you can hold the steering wheel comfortably. If you are too far back, you will tend to hunch your shoulders forward. Most people's tendency when traffic gets bad is to lean forward toward the wheel. Remember to keep your body supported against the seat and lengthened. Allow your hands to hold the wheel lightly but firmly, and avoid gripping the wheel with excess tension. (See Figure 35.)

It's healthy to avoid elevators when possible and take advantage of the exercise that going up and down stairs provides. As with so many other movements, it is common to see people hunching over or hyperextending their backs when they go up stairs. Most often they are unconsciously trying to lift themselves up with their backs. What brings you up the stairs is your legs and the momentum of the movement. Direct yourself to maintain good body use as you go up. Allow your knees to extend all the way forward and let your feet come down lightly on the stairs rather than pushing your whole body down into each stair. Although it is tempting to let your body scrunch downward as you walk down stairs, remember that you want your body to release upward even though you are traveling downward in space. Let each downward step remind you to release upward. Let your hand glide lightly along the handrail rather than gripping it tightly. (See Figure 36.)

USING THE STAIRS ✑

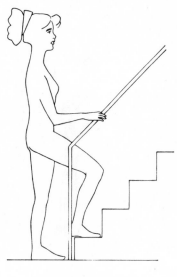

Figure 36

Since a doorknob is below you, and it is habitual to let your body go down when your hand goes down, inhibit the desire to pull toward the door. Allow yourself to stay back and up away from the door as your hand reaches the doorknob. Make sure that your shoulder doesn't hunch forward when you pull the door toward you, and continue to direct yourself as the door comes toward you. (See Figure 37.) If the door is very heavy, think of opening it with your whole torso and body rather than with just your hand and arm. If you are a small person facing a large door, you may want to use leverage by placing your other hand on the wall next to the door and pushing in as you open the door. If you are pushing a heavy door away from you, lean your body weight toward the door to help open it.

OPENING A DOOR ✑

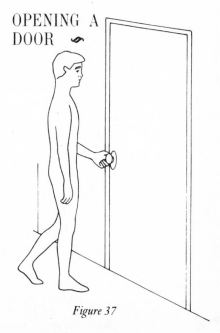

Figure 37

STANDING FOR A LONG PERIOD ∽

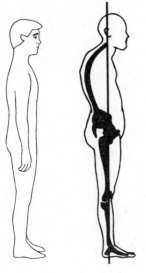

Figure 38   *Figure 39*

There will be times when you have to stand for a long period of time: standing in line at the bank, post office, or grocery store; standing room at the theater, sporting events, or music events. Your poor body habits tend to become exaggerated when you are still for long periods, either sitting or standing. The key thing to remember is that the body is never absolutely still. Even when you are asleep your ribs move in and out with your breathing. When you have to stand for a long time, don't think of yourself as static: Be aware of your directions and your breathing and the movement of your ribs. If you are free in your legs at the ankle, knee, and hip joints, then you will sway very slightly as you breathe. We don't have four solid supports underneath us like a chair or a table; we are "teetering bipeds," animals that have only two legs, so instability is built into our structure. If you tense your legs you will be still, but your breathing will become shallow and your torso tight. If you are free in your legs and thinking your directions, you will move very, very slightly. The World Trade Center towers sway back and forth twenty feet in wind—they have to. If a big storm hit and the towers didn't have freedom of movement, they would be damaged. We, too, need to be free to move gently. (See Figures 38 and 39.)

LIFTING HEAVY OBJECTS ∽

The tendency when lifting something heavy is to anticipate the weight of the object and prepare to lift it by oversupporting, which causes tightening. Tension has weight, so when you pick up the object, not only are you lifting the weight of the object, but also the weight of the tension. Rather than anticipating the weight of the object, therefore, let your body decide how much support is necessary in the process. The weight of the object should be evenly distributed throughout your body, so that no one area (such as your shoulders or lower back) does most of the work. Use the instructions for bending when lifting something heavy. It is very important that you bend at the knees and hips when you lift so that the lower back is not strained, but make sure you do this with direction. Don't be foolhardy—if something is too heavy for you, get someone to help you. Straining your back is not worth it.

Some people are very uncomfortable sitting on the floor and should not try it. Others find the floor the most comfortable place to sit. To make it easier to maintain your spinal length, sit crosslegged on a pillow: Your buttocks are on the pillow, your legs are not. Sitting in this way is easier than sitting directly on the floor. (See Figure 40.) You can also try sitting on your haunches with a pillow under your hips, although this way is more difficult for most people.

SITTING ON THE FLOOR ✍

Figure 40

Often people bend over from the waist and hunch their shoulders in order to push a vacuum or pull a rake. It is easy to misuse yourself by flinging your arms away, breaking in the middle of your back, or tightening your shoulders. It is also common to pull your limbs in too tightly when pulling the rake or vacuum toward the body. Try using the lunge instead. When you have to push the vacuum away from your body, let your head, neck, and torso constitute an integrated unit that is long and wide. Your arms should extend as you bend your forward knee and leave your back leg straight. That way your body stays in a straight line. The same relationship should exist

RAKING AND VACUUMING ✍

Figure 41

Applying the Leibowitz Procedures to Daily Activities

between your head, neck, and torso as when you are standing upright. The movement of pulling and pushing is facilitated by the movement of the lunge forward and back. (See Figure 41.) The lunge is also a wonderful tool to use while raking. You can lunge in any direction—forward, sideways, and backward. When done well it looks like a beautiful tai chi dance or advanced fencing (in slow motion, of course).

CARRYING PURSES, BRIEFCASES, AND BAGS ✍

People with back trouble should avoid carrying heavy objects if possible. Shoulder bags should be small, with straps that can be worn diagonally across the body to keep the weight as even as possible on all parts of the body. (See Figure 42.) Be sure to alternate between shoulders. Briefcases can be carried in the same manner if they have straps. Put only what is absolutely necessary into your bags. If you must carry large bags (because you carry a lot of books or exercise clothing, for example) you might try a backpack. Backpacks keep the weight even across your shoulders. But make sure it hangs on a part of your back that is comfortable. Sometimes backpacks encourage people to hunch forward, so remember to keep your spine lengthened when you have it on. Don't let the weight of the shoulder bag or backpack pull you down toward the floor—think up against it.

If you are not comfortable with your purse or briefcase lying diagonally across your body, then carry it on one shoulder or in your hand. The problem now is that one side of your body has weight pulling down on it and the other doesn't. Your body should not give in to the downward pull by sagging down or by displacing one hip out to the side. Your body should remain centered with the bag hanging straight down. If you have a purse hanging on your shoulder, make

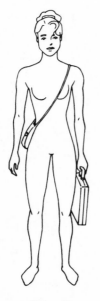

Figure 42

THE LEIBOWITZ PROCEDURES

sure not to hunch your shoulders forward or push them too far back. Rest your hand lightly on the purse or strap to keep it in place; that way you don't have to tense the shoulder to keep the strap from falling off. The same principles hold true if you are carrying luggage, although we recommend that you get luggage with wheels on it. If you have back problems, then luggage with wheels is a must.

Figure 43

If you have to carry a heavy object in front of you, like a grocery bag, you must move back to compensate for the extra weight in front. Most people lean back from the waist, which puts a great deal of pressure on the lower back. Instead, let your whole body lean slightly back from your ankle joints, as this will effectively compensate for the weight in front. (See Figure 43.)

Ordinarily your rib cage will move forward and your lower back will arch when you reach for something above you. You may feel as though this arching is helping you reach higher, but you can actually reach farther if your rib cage and lower back are in line with the rest of your torso. Your arm and shoulder can then stretch away from your torso. If you maintain good body use and simply come up onto your toes by gently pressing the balls of your feet down while reaching up with your arm, you will be able to reach quite far without undue effort.

REACHING FOR AN OBJECT ON A HIGH SHELF ✎

In complex movement activities like housecleaning or washing the car, you will need to use almost every procedure covered in the last chapter. You will probably have to squat, bend, reach, lift, stretch, lunge,

HOUSECLEANING AND WASHING THE CAR ✎

and possibly go onto your hands and knees. Try not to get so involved in the activity that you lose all sense of yourself. It's sometimes easy to forget good body use when you're scrubbing something hard, attempting to get it clean. If you give attention to how you are moving and reaching, these activities can turn from tiresome chores into explorations of your own movement. Instead of feeling tired and drained at the end, you can feel as though you have had a physical stretch and workout.

GARDENING &

Gardening provides great opportunities either to hurt yourself or to promote spinal lengthening. Done poorly, many of the activities involved in gardening can be harmful to your back: Weeding while bending from the waist, shoveling dirt or manure while slouching, and planting seeds with tensed shoulders and arms are some examples. Conversely, if you weed while squatting or crawling on all fours, gardening can be very beneficial for your back: Bending properly while shoveling can be very good exercise. Make sure that you let your legs do the work, keep your torso lengthening, and don't contract your shoulders. The bending, stretching, and reaching involved in gardening can be excellent exercise as long as you follow your directions.

EATING &

The guidelines given for sitting also apply to sitting at a table to eat. Depending on what you are eating, you may sit upright in the chair with your chair close to the table and use the back of the chair for support, or you may lean forward from the hip joints if you are eating something that could easily spill (like soup or pasta). Often people pull their bodies down to the food rather than bringing the food up to their mouths. Thinking your directions, let your fingers lead the utensil up to your mouth. (See Figure 44.) Let your fingers, wrist, and shoulder be free as you do so. At first this may feel as though the fork has to travel an awfully long way to get to your mouth, or it may feel formal compared to the way you usually eat, but you will get used to it in time. When you drink, rather than slumping down to bring your mouth to the glass, bring the glass slightly above your mouth. You can now tip your head back and tip the glass up without compressing your neck.

Figure 44

SLEEPING

A firm mattress is best for supporting your body while sleeping, but it should be comfortable. If you sleep on your back, use a pillow under your head and one or two under your knees. If you sleep on your side, use a pillow under your head and neck. You may also want to use another pillow between your knees or at your stomach to support your lower back. If you sleep on your stomach, bend one leg and place a pillow under your stomach to support your lower back and your bent leg side. Since your head is twisted in this position, don't place a pillow under your head, or if you are uncomfortable without a pillow, use a thin soft one.

Applying the Leibowitz Procedures to Sports and Exercise ∞

The news media tell us we are in the middle of an exercise revolution, and it's true that more people have a strenuous, regular exercise routine than in the past. Yet while some are involved with vigorous exercise such as aerobics several times a week or running tens of miles, recent research shows that many more are completely sedentary or are active only sporadically. Whether people are very active or never move from their easy chairs, many are interested in the subject. We are often asked for our thoughts on the various forms of exercises. In this chapter we briefly discuss the most popular forms of exercise. We do not claim to be experts on the subject of sports, but we can point out what you should be aware of in yourself when you are exercising.

The research shows that the most dramatic increase in fitness comes from getting people who are completely sedentary to do simple exercises, such as walking. So if you are inactive, we recommend that you walk whenever possible, abandon the elevator and take the stairs when you can, run with your dog in the park, and so on. In other words, we believe in moving and using the body as often as possible and in natural and pleasurable ways. A body that is active responds more quickly to the Alexander Technique.

But whether you walk for exercise or are a championship athlete, it is important to use your body well during physical activity. To use yourself well you should take special care to apply the Alexander principles when exercising; you will then end up using what in sports is called "good form." If you are doing any type of sport or exercise using excess muscle tension, your capacity to do the exercise well will be limited and you may even hurt yourself because of it. A good example is lifting weights. You can go into any health club that has weights and see people bending themselves all out of shape when engaged in this activity. Many people use weights that are too heavy for them and strain their whole body to lift the weight. The same thing applies to other forms of exercise: Pushing yourself too long or too hard can lead to injury.

Another common phenomenon is the "weekend athlete," someone who was physically active during high school and college and because of career or personal demands is unable to stay active except on occasion. The weekend athlete's body goes from being completely sedentary to being exercised vigorously, often with no warm-up or stretching beforehand. This is the perfect setup for personal injury. The more out of shape you are, the greater the chance for muscle pains and strains. Often these weekend athletes are young—in their thirties and forties—and remember clearly the physical strength and mobility that they had in the recent past. This can lead them to push themselves beyond where they should go.

There are now many books on the market that

emphasize not only the correct form of a sport but a general attitude with which to approach the learning of it. Books such as *Centered Riding* and *Centered Skiing* explain how you can release your body and maintain that freedom as you pursue the sport. These books are generally helpful, and you should refer to them when learning. If you are taking classes in any of these physical activities, make sure you are comfortable with the teacher. Teachers should be knowledgeable about the body and how it works, should be open to questions, and should never push you beyond where you can go. Making a student push for results can easily lead to excessive muscle tension and strain and can sometimes pave the way for injury. Exercise caution in choosing a teacher when you are exercising your body. Also, remember to stretch and warm up before exercising and to stretch and cool down afterward. This will only take a few minutes, but it is extremely important in helping to prevent injury and overtightening of your muscles.

WEIGHT LIFTING ✍ Many people now belong to health clubs and spend several hours a week lifting free weights or using the different types of resistance machines. Since this is a time when you are focusing on yourself, it's a wonderful opportunity to apply the Alexander principles. When lifting weights or using the machines, make sure that you are using the correct muscles to do the exercise. Understand what the objective of each exercise is and which muscles should be working in it. If you are not clear, ask your trainer or consult a good training manual.

The objective in lifting weights is to strengthen specific muscles. You have to stress the muscle if you want to increase its strength, so the idea is to begin lifting a weight that is easy for you to lift, then slowly increase the weight so that your strength and/or muscle bulk increases. In an effort to achieve quick results, people often start with a weight that is too heavy for them or increase the weight too quickly. When the weight is too heavy, the lifter tends to compensate by using not only the muscles that are supposed to be working, but also auxiliary muscles to help out. This often reduces the work load on the muscles that are supposed to be working, thereby undermining the whole purpose of the exercise. In addition, proper form is generally lost when the weight is too heavy, so you see people using their shoulder muscles to lift weights that are supposed to be lifted by the biceps.

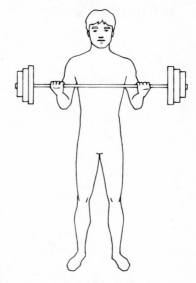

Figure 45

It is better to use a weight that you know you can lift without undue strain and make sure you are using only the muscles that are supposed to be working. Then you can slowly add weight, carefully checking in the mirror that you aren't losing your form just because you are adding weight. This may take longer, but it is much safer and more effective in the long run. Do not anticipate the weight by preparing with tension. Your objective should be to work with your whole body, keeping it lengthened and free with the head poised, so that you can more effectively work on specific muscles. Only by working with the whole mind/body can this be achieved. (See Figure 45.)

In weight lifting it is essential to stretch your whole body before and after exercising. Weight lifting without stretching can lead to tightness and restriction at the joints, which will impair the free movement of your body.

AEROBICS ✍

This type of exercise is very popular, especially with women. We do not recommend high-impact aerobics because they are simply too difficult for most people to do without hurting themselves. The constant jumping and hopping in place can jar your joints and back, especially if your club doesn't have a proper wooden or sprung floor. Dancers require a wooden floor to dance safely—cement is dangerous to the hips, knees, and ankle joints—but aerobic studios often have cement floors covered by carpets, and carpets are not enough to safely cushion your body.

Low-impact aerobics are easier on your body because you always have one foot on the floor, which greatly reduces the impact on your body. Even with low-impact aerobics, however, your club should have a wooden floor. As with any exercise, it's alright to test your limits and work constantly toward improving, but make sure the class is at your level so that you won't be either bored or pushing yourself too hard to keep up. Try several different classes until you find a teacher who doesn't push you beyond where you can go and who has knowledge of body use and alignment.

Unless you use your body well when exercising, the exercise won't do you any good. In fact, if your body use is poor, in some cases the exercises can prove harmful. Therefore it's important to keep your whole body in mind rather than just the part that's working.

WALKING ✍

Walking is gentle but effective exercise. To obtain the best results, walk briskly for twenty minutes at least three times a week. Allow your arms to swing. There will be a slight swaying through your hip area as well. Think your directions as you walk and remember to maintain the upward release. Walking is not strenuous and allows you to maintain good body use with ease. All you need is a pair of walking shoes that will give your feet support.

SWIMMING ✍

Swimming is a safe exercise that is often recommended by medical professionals for individuals who have back problems. Try to vary your strokes to insure that certain body parts do not become overdeveloped. Make sure that you maintain good form, especially when doing the breast stroke, which requires that you raise your head out of the water so that you can easily overtighten your neck. Also be aware of leaving your neck free as you turn your head back and forth in the crawl. (See Figure 46.) The back stroke is especially healthy since when lying on your back you are less likely to strain. Allow the water to support your body weight. The water provides enough resistance to exercise your whole body. You may also wish to do exercises at the edge of the pool.

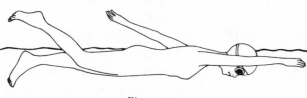

Figure 46

BIKING ✍

If you have a bike with curled-under handlebars, maintain your body freedom in the curled over position. Don't hunch over, but think your directions as you gently let your body form the shape of a C curve, which is very different from slumping. Don't tense your shoulders unnecessarily. Although your head will have to be tilted slightly back when you're riding a racing bike, make sure that you don't overtighten your neck to maintain this position. Let your spine lengthen upward and your knees release forward as you pedal. (See Figure 47.) You may want to sit erect occasionally and ride with your hands on top of the handlebars to give your back a change. Some people find it more comfortable to ride bikes that allow them to sit upright.

Figure 47

RUNNING

Figure 48

Running is a very strenuous activity that puts a good deal of pressure on your back, hips, knees, ankle joints, and feet. With each running step, two-and-a-half times your body weight comes down on your joints. We strongly recommend that you do not run on asphalt or concrete. No matter how good your shoes are and how good your form is, we feel running on these surfaces puts too much strain on the human body. If you do run, run on a good track, the grass, or sand. As with walking, let your knees move forward as your body lengthens upward. Let your arms move freely with your body motion. (See Figure 48.) Some people find race-walking a satisfying alternative to running. Let your knees release forward as your spine releases up, and remain free in your hip sockets so that your hips can make the exaggerated hip motion.

When addressing the ball, use the procedures listed earlier for bending. Do not bend over from your waist; instead, incline your body forward from your hip joints. Make sure you don't hunch your shoulders forward when bringing the club to the ball. It is important that your torso remain lengthened and widened as you rotate to swing. This is a very strong motion and should take place throughout your torso rather than in an isolated part of your back. (See Figure 49.) If you consistently twist your body at one specific point rather than through the whole mechanism, you are setting yourself up for back trouble.

GOLF

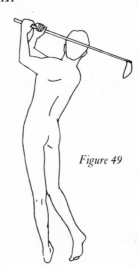

Figure 49

Again, the bending procedures are easily applied to tennis. Don't hunch over from your waist or shoulders as you play. Let your body lengthen upward, and think of the racket as an extension of your arm. Through much of the game you will be bent at the ankle, knee, and hip joints and will incline slightly forward. (See Figure 50.) This is a position of great power. If the muscles of your torso lengthen and widen, you will have more power and flexibility in your strokes and will be able to move more quickly and efficiently in any direction.

TENNIS

Figure 50

Whether you are studying tap, jazz, ballet, modern dance, creative movement, or contact improvisation, dance classes also provide an excellent opportunity to apply your Alexander directions. The freedom and flexibility that are necessary in dance will be enhanced by using the Alexander principles. They help the free

DANCING

flow of energy through your muscles and joints and can help free your imagination as well.

SKIING ✍

Skiing requires that you lengthen your torso while bending your knees. You should also be free at the hip joints so that you can rotate back and forth as you travel down the slopes. (See Figure 51.) The bending procedures outlined earlier can be directly applied to this activity. You may wish to practice the bending procedures while bouncing slightly in place to simulate the action of skiing downhill. Your legs should be free and easy and ready to move in any direction.

Figure 51

RIDING ✍

Riding is an interesting activity in that you have to deal with both yourself and another animal. Dressage teaches principles that reinforce the Alexander principles. The more freedom you have in your body and the more sensitivity you have in your hands as they

THE LEIBOWITZ PROCEDURES

hold the reins, the more control you will have over the horse. If you are tense, your horse will feel it through your legs, feet, hands, and even through your seat on the saddle. Lengthening and widening will keep you free and able to move with your horse. (See Figure 52.)

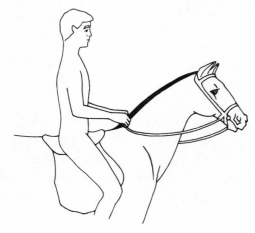

Figure 52

Yoga is a series of stretching exercises, some of which place you in positions that you would not otherwise get into in your daily life. Some of them have to be maintained for a long period of time. The Alexander directions will help you move unusual ways and will give you feedback as to whether everything is alright in that unusual position. (See Figure 53.) Never force yourself in any of the exercises; take it slow and easy, and make sure that you don't hold your breath.

YOGA

Figure 53

Conclusion ✑

The Alexander Technique is a tool for living. In addition to helping you with difficulties that you may currently have, it is a preventive instrument that can aid you in avoiding future problems. In helping your mind and body to work well together in a unified manner, you are predisposing yourself to health and well-being. If you choose to learn it, the Alexander Technique can be used to solve a specific body misuse problem, or can be used as a means to enhance your life in all its facets. Working with it is an ongoing process, and you decide how far you will go.

F. M. Alexander described the process best when he wrote:

> It is my belief, confirmed by the research and practice of nearly twenty years, that man's supreme inheritance of conscious guidance and control is within the grasp of anyone who will take the trouble to cultivate it. . . . It is no esoteric doctrine or mystical cult, but a synthesis of entirely reasonable propositions that can be demonstrated in pure theory and substantiated in common practice. . . .
>
> It is essential that the peoples of civilization should comprehend the value of

their inheritance, the outcome of the long process of evolution which will enable them to govern the uses of their own physical mechanisms. . . . This triumph is not to be won in sleep, in trance, in submission, in paralysis, or in anesthesia, but in a clear, open-eyed, reasoning, deliberate consciousness and apprehension of the wonderful potentialities possessed by mankind, the transcendent inheritance of a conscious mind.*

Ultimately, the Alexander Technique will help you deal with any life situation. To accomplish this you must give yourself the most important gift you can give to yourself: time. It takes time to incorporate the technique into your life. But if you take the time and direct your energies to learning the Alexander Technique, you will not only change in ways that you want but also discover new and unexpected beneficial changes in your life.

* Alexander, F. M. *Man's Supreme Inheritance*. London: Re-Educational Publications Limited, 1946.

Suggested Reading List 〜

BOOKS ON THE
ALEXANDER
TECHNIQUE ∾

Alexander, F. M. *Constructive Conscious Control of the Individual*. Long Beach, Calif.: Centerline Press, 1985. Introduction by Walter Carrington. (First published in 1923 by E. P. Dutton, New York, with an introduction by John Dewey.)

You may find reading Alexander's prose tough going at times, but it is worth it to find the gems. This book describes his technique and how it works and covers topics such as breathing, the mechanisms of fear reflexes, imitation, concentration, memory, and feeling.

———. *The Use of the Self*. Long Beach, Calif.: Centerline Press, 1985. Preface by Marjorie Barstow. (First published in 1932 by E. P. Dutton, New York, with an introduction by John Dewey.)

The most understandable of Alexander's books, it chronicles the development of his technique over a long period and includes case studies from his practice that illustrate how the technique can help people.

Caplan, Deborah. *Back Trouble: A New Approach to Prevention and Recovery Based on the Alexander Technique*. Gainesville, Fla.: Triad Publishing Company, 1987.

This valuable book gives exercises developed by an Alexander teacher and physical therapist that are designed to reduce and prevent pain.

Pierce Jones, Frank. *Body Awareness in Action*. New York: Schocken Books, 1976.

Written by an Alexander teacher who was trained by F. M. Alexander and his brother A. R. Alexander, it includes his personal experiences in the technique as well as the results of experiments he conducted with multiple image photography and electromyograms. These experiments document what happens in the body when the Alexander Technique is used.

Maisel, Edward, ed. *The Alexander Technique: The Essential Writings of F. Matthias Alexander*. New York: University Books, Carol Communications, 1989. (Formerly titled "Resurrection of the Body.")

A book of selected writings from Alexander's four books. It is well organized and contains interesting background information on Alexander's life.

Sanfilippo, Phyllis. *The Reader's Guide to the Alexander Technique: A Selected Annotated Bibliography*. Long Beach, Calif.: Centerline Press, 1987.

Many of these books are available through Centerline Press, 2005 Palo Verde Avenue, Suite 325, Long Beach, CA 90815.

BOOKS ON RELATED TOPICS ✑

Asimov, Isaac. *The Human Body: Its Structure and Operation*. New York: New American Library, 1963.

An easy-to-understand book that explains the structure and function of the human body.

Herrigel, Eugen. *Zen in the Art of Archery*. New York: Vintage Books, 1971.

A magnificent book that describes the way of Zen. It chronicles one man's journey in learning this physical and spiritual discipline. It describes how to learn a difficult skill while maintaining ease and poise.

Kapit, Wynn, and Lawrence M. Elson. *The Anatomy Coloring Book*. New York: Harper & Row, 1977.

A fun way to learn more about anatomy.

Miller, Jonathan. *The Body in Question*. New York: Random House, 1982.

An unusual and intelligent look at the structure and operation of the human body.

Index 〜

About the Authors ∽

JUDITH LEIBOWITZ studied the Alexander Technique privately and trained as an Alexander teacher with Lulie Westfeldt and Alma Frank. She received further instruction from F. M. Alexander. In 1964 she co-founded the American Center for the Alexander Technique and was director of its teacher certification program until 1981. She continues to teach in the program and is responsible for the training of nearly half of the country's certified teachers.

In 1968 John Houseman invited her to join the Drama Department faculty at The Juilliard School. She continues to be a member of the faculty. She has introduced and/or taught the Alexander Technique at the American Conservatory Theatre in San Francisco, the Arena Stage in Washington, D.C., Temple University in Philadelphia, the Kristin Linklater Voice Teacher's Training Program in New York, the Shakespeare Festival in Stratford, Ontario, and at other schools across the country.

She has taught many of the country's well-known actors and is one of the world's leading authorities on the Alexander Technique. She has a private practice in New York City.

BILL CONNINGTON is president and chairman of the board of the American Center for the Alexander Technique and a former associate faculty member. He is on the faculty of The Juilliard School, has taught the technique at universities and performing arts conservatories across the United States, and is in private practice in New York City. He is a graduate of the American Center for the Alexander Technique and trained as an actor at the London Academy of Music and Dramatic Art.